MARY FORD'S
NEW BOOK OF
CAKE
DECORATING

MARY FORD'S
NEW BOOK OF
CAKE
DECORATING

MARY FORD

A MARY FORD BOOK

Typesetting by Avant Mode Limited, Bournemouth.

Printed in Hong Kong, produced by Mandarin Offset Limited.

ISBN 0 946429 59 6

THE AUTHOR

The name of Mary Ford has become synonymous with the very highest quality in traditional and modern cake decoration.

Widely acknowledged as one of the U.K.'s most innovative designers and cake artists, Mary has taught for over 25 years and her range of books have become required reading for cake decorators across the world.

Mary's warmth and unique practical style of teaching shines through this book. The easy to use and friendly approach, imaginative use of illustrations and numerous colour photographs together with Mary's simple step by step procedures make even the most difficult cake design accessible.

Mary introduces the basic methods, builds confidence steadily and progresses naturally to the more advanced techniques. Finally, her aim is to fire your own imagination using your newly acquired skills.

As with all the other titles in the Mary Ford series, this book is the result of a close collaboration between Mary and her husband Michael who is both photographer and executive director.

Mary Ford stresses the importance of all aspects of cake artistry, but gives special emphasis to the basic ingredients and unreservedly recommends the use of Tate & Lyle cane sugar.

Mary Ford acknowledges with grateful thanks the assistance of Mary Smith and Dawn Pennington in creating some of the items and cakes featured in this book.

CONTENTS

NOTE: WHEN MAKING ANY OF THE RECIPES IN
THIS BOOK, FOLLOW ONE SET OF MEASUREMENTS
ONLY AS THEY ARE NOT INTERCHANGEABLE.

INTRODUCTION

"The Mary Ford Book of Cake Decorating" is the most comprehensive book on cake decorating and design that I have produced to date. This step by step guide will take you from the basic essentials to some of the most advanced modern sugar artistry techniques.

As with all the books in the Mary Ford series, my emphasis is on developing your craftsmanship and practical skills. This new book will meet the ever increasing demand from colleges, cake artistry schools and cake decorators for a key reference manual.

I have included cake designs and decorations that are suitable for all levels of skill and experience. All the designs can be adapted to form the basis of a cake which reflects your own personal skills and creative ability. Using the detailed index and glossary, it is a simple matter to locate the relevant recipe, technique or guidance.

Colour photographs illustrate every stage of the decorating process and the introductory section covers the basics of equipment and preparation, with recipes and techniques laid out for easy reference.

Think of any happy occasion and you will find a beautifully decorated cake to celebrate it in the pages that follow. That is one of the pleasures of our hobby, it celebrates the joyful moments of life. Weddings, christenings, birthdays, anniversaries and so on. You will find imaginative designs suitable for all these occasions, and more, in this book.

You will also discover designs that range from the simple to the elaborate. Designs which really allow you to develop your skills, and experienced decorators will be challenged by the creative and innovative ideas outlined in the more advanced designs.

I am often asked what are the secrets of cake artistry. I always respond that my many years of teaching cake design and decoration have taught me that time, patience and practice are the cornerstones of success.

As with most things, it is always best to start at the beginning. I strongly recommend that you read through the preliminary pages which demonstrate

the preparation and coating of cakes. Beginners will soon find that, by developing the simple techniques such as buttercream, they will have the basis of a rewarding pastime. More experienced practitioners will discover advice on design and colour as well as advanced and innovative techniques.

Planning and organisation are also very important. For example, fruit cakes

need time to mature while almond paste and coatings have to dry before decorating can begin. Many decorative items should be prepared in advance and stored until required. A rich cake should be completed at least two to three days before use, whereas a sponge should be made as late as possible to ensure freshness.

Precious time can be saved by the use of readily available items such as silk, artificial and crystallised flowers. Royal iced items are fragile so it is worth making more pieces, such as collars and lace, than are required so that breakages do not halt progress unnecessarily. Reading my useful hints and tips will avoid any unnecessary disappointment.

It is always worth taking the time to practice the design first as this can avoid wasting hours of preparation on the basic coated cake. An upturned cake tin or any flat, clean surface, makes a useful dummy on which to work and this is particularly useful when experimenting with, and incorporating aspects from, different cakes into your finished design.

Please do remember that no matter how beautiful the finished design, if the cake itself is not perfect, the whole exercise has been fruitless. For that reason I have included in the preliminary section of the book some tried and tested cake recipes to ensure success.

I hope that this book will stimulate your imagination and help you further develop your skills and expertise in this rewarding hobby of cake decoration and design.

MARY FORD

EQUIPMENT

There is no doubt that the right equipment makes cake decorating much easier. However, it is always possible to improvise and still achieve excellent results.

The first rule when buying is to look for quality. It would be a shame to see your hard work spoilt by equipment that contaminates the ingredients. If you buy carefully, not only will your utensils last a lifetime, but they will not rust, bend or chip.

Always use food-approved spoons and plastic bowls and, if possible, you should keep these utensils only for cake decorating. Remember that all metal utensils, other than stainless steel, are unsuitable as they discolour icing. Glass and earthenware containers are perfect although you must ensure that they do not have any cracks where grease lurks. Cake tins come in a wide variety of sizes and shapes but should always be strong and rigid. It is also worth spending money on good quality greaseproof paper which will avoid unnecessary problems in baking and decorating.

A decorating turntable makes all the difference when working on a cake and a small one may be easily improvised using an upturned cake tin or plate. However, a proper turntable is an essential investment if you are going to do a lot of decorating and really will make the task much easier. Look for a turntable that is capable of supporting a heavy cake and still turns easily when in use. It should also have a non-slip base and a minimum diameter of 23cm (9in).

Rolling pins are essential tools for the cake decorator. You will need a good quality one that is smooth and heavy for rolling out pastes (about 45cm or 18in long). Nylon spacers achieve an even thickness of paste. Smaller plastic rolling pins will also be useful.

A variety of stainless steel palette knives are required for mixing-in colour and coating cakes. A 18cm (7in) and a 10cm (4in) will probably be enough to cope with most tasks. You will also need a stainless steel or rigid plastic straight edge that is at least 38cm (15in) long for smoothing royal icing and buttercream. This can be improvised using a stainless steel ruler if necessary.

Coating the sides of cakes is best done with purpose made rigid plastic or stainless steel side scrapers. Piping tubes may be plastic or metal and come in a wide variety of different sizes (see page 31). It is important to wash out piping tubes

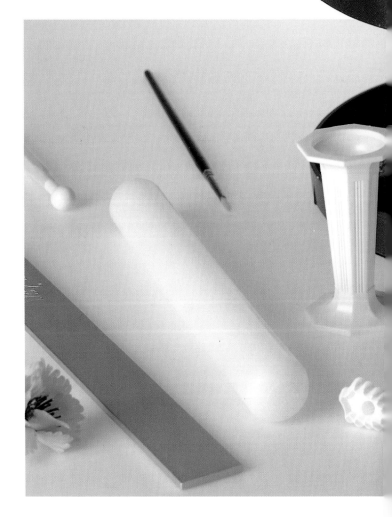

immediately after use to prevent the icing hardening inside. Flower cutters, crimpers and other specialised equipment are available from most sugarcraft shops.

Before baking or decorating a cake, make sure you have all the equipment and ingredients ready and easily to hand. Be absolutely certain that all utensils and equipment are scrupulously clean and free from grease. An electric mixer will prove to be a great bonus and will save time and energy although it is by no means essential for success.

ACKNOWLEDGEMENTS

With grateful thanks to:

CAKEBOARDS LIMITED, 47-53 Dace Road, London E3 2NH, England. Manufacturers and suppliers of cake decorating equipment and decorations to the Wholesale and Retail Trade.

ORCHARD PRODUCTS, 51 Hallyburton Road, Hove, East Sussex BN3 7GP, England. Manufacturers and suppliers of cake decorating equipment to the Retail Trade and by Mail Order.

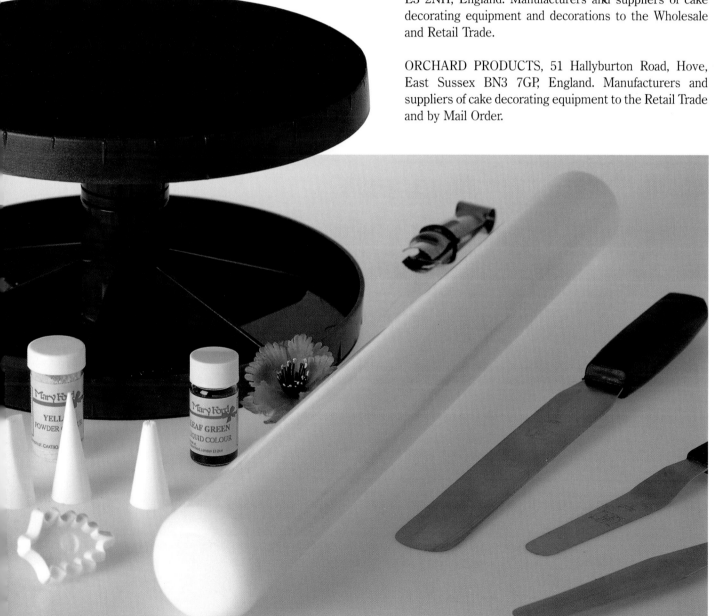

HINTS AND TIPS

BUTTERCREAM

When making buttercream use only fresh butter that is at a temperature of 18-21℃ (65-70°F).
Adding too much colouring to buttercream can make it strong and bitter so add a few drops at a time, tasting between additions.

CAKES and SPONGES

Many of the designs in this book are suitable for both sponge and fruit cakes.
Unusually shaped tins for special occasion cakes may be purchased or hired.

CURDLING

Curdling can occur if eggs are added too quickly to the cake mixture or if there is insufficient beating between the additions. If curdling does occur, immediately beat in a small amount of flour until the batter is smooth and then continue adding egg, a little at a time. Should curdling re-occur simply add a little more flour.

FIXING

Apricot purée can be used to fix cake to cake or almond paste to cake. Buttercream can be used to join sponge cakes.
Always use cooled, boiled water or clear liquor when fixing sugarpaste to sugarpaste.
Use royal icing to fix royal icing or runouts.
Ribbons should be fixed with small dots or fine lines of royal icing.

FREEZING

Batch baked swiss rolls and sponges can be frozen for up to six months. Swiss rolls should be rolled up before freezing and stored unfilled. Make sure that they are completely thawed before unrolling and filling.

PIPING GEL

Most sugarcraft outlets stock clear piping gel which may be easily coloured using liquid or paste food colourings. Many supermarkets also stock ready made tubes of coloured piping gel.
Use a small piping bag without a tube for piping. Do not overfill the bag. Outline each section with royal icing before filling with piping gel. A little piping gel can go a very long way.

PIPING ROYAL ICING

Use an upturned cake tin to practice on.
Always pipe onto a dry surface.
Piped work must always be dry before starting overpiping.

PORTIONS

A 20.5cm (8in) round sponge provides about 16 portions.
A 20.5cm (8in) round fruit cake provides about 40 portions and a square cake provides about 54 portions.

ROYAL ICING

Royal icing should always have a clean glossy appearance, good white colour and a light texture.

When making royal icing, add the icing sugar slowly and then beat well to avoid a grainy texture.

Under-mixed royal icing has a creamy look and should be beaten further.

Always make up sufficient coloured icing as it will almost be impossible to match the colour later.

Cover bowls of royal icing with a clean, damp cloth to prevent drying out.

Stipple royal icing using a clean household sponge or palette knife.

SUGARPASTE

Sugarpaste may be purchased ready-made if required.

Always make sugarpaste 24 hours before use and store in a cool place (not a refrigerator) using an airtight container.

Use edible food colouring to colour sugarpaste. Add a very small amount of the required colour to the paste using a cocktail stick or skewer.

Knead the paste thoroughly until the colour is mixed evenly and then roll out the paste to ensure that there is no streaking.

Mottled sugarpaste can be made by half mixing with the required colour before rolling out the paste.

Always produce enough coloured sugarpaste for your needs as it is virtually impossible to match the same colour later.

Coloured sugarpaste should be protected from strong light.

Flavour sugarpaste to counteract sweetness by using peppermint, orange, vanilla etc.

Add a little vegetable fat or egg white if the paste is too dry.

Sugarpaste should be rolled out on an icing sugar or cornflour dusted surface. Icing sugar gives a matt finish while cornflour gives a satin finish.

Always warm sugarpaste slightly if cold before use.

The drying time for sugarpaste is approximately 24 hours but may vary according to moisture in the air.

To crimp, push the crimper gently into the paste before squeezing the crimper. Carefully release pressure and remove crimper.

When making frills, always place the tapered end of the cocktail stick over the edge of the thinly rolled sugarpaste. Rock the stick back and forth covering a small area at a time. If too sticky, add a little cornflour.

TIMING

Always carefully read through the information on your selected cake design before you start. Check exactly what is required and then work backwards from the date the cake is needed so you can plan a timing schedule. Enough time must be allowed for fruit cakes to mature, coatings and piping to dry, together with the necessary items to be purchased.

It takes about three weeks for a rich fruit cake to mature.

ALL-IN-ONE FRUIT CAKE

This fruit cake makes the ideal base for any sugarpaste or royal icing celebration cake and has excellent keeping properties. When making a fruit cake, it requires at least three weeks to mature.
For hexagonal, octagonal or petal shaped cakes use recipe for the equivalent round cake. Example, for 20.5cm (8in) heart shape use ingredients for 20.5cm (8in) round cake.

Square tin	12.5cm (5in)	15cm (6in)	18cm (7in)	20.5cm (8in)	23cm (9in)	25.5cm (10in)	28cm (11in)
OR							
Round tin	15cm (6in)	18cm (7in)	20.5cm (8in)	23cm (9in)	25.5cm (10in)	28cm (11in)	30.5cm (12in)
Sultanas	85g (3oz)	115g (4oz)	170g (6oz)	225g (8oz)	285g (10oz)	340g (12oz)	425g (15oz)
Currants	85g (3oz)	115g (4oz)	170g (6oz)	225g (8oz)	285g (10oz)	340g (12oz)	425g (15oz)
Raisins	85g (3oz)	115g (4oz)	170g (6oz)	225g (8oz)	285g (10oz)	340g (12oz)	425g (15oz)
Candied peel	30g (1oz)	60g (2oz)	60g (2oz)	85g (3oz)	85g (3oz)	115g (4oz)	170g (6oz)
Glacé cherries	30g (1oz)	60g (2oz)	60g (2oz)	85g (3oz)	85g (3oz)	115g (4oz)	170g (6oz)
Lemon rind (lemons)	¼	½	½	1	1½	2	2
Rum/Brandy	½tbsp	½tbsp	1tbsp	1tbsp	1½tbsp	2tbsp	2tbsp
Black treacle	½tbsp	½tbsp	1tbsp	1tbsp	1½tbsp	2tbsp	2tbsp
Soft (tub) margarine	85g (3oz)	115g (4oz)	170g (6oz)	225g (8oz)	285g (10oz)	340g (12oz)	425g (15oz)
Soft light brown sugar	85g (3oz)	115g (4oz)	170g (6oz)	225g (8oz)	285g (10oz)	340g (12oz)	425g (15oz)
Eggs, size 3	1½	2	3	4	5	6	7½
Ground almonds	15g (½oz)	30g (1oz)	45g (1½oz)	60g (2oz)	70g (2½oz)	85g (3oz)	115g (4oz)
Self-raising flour	115g (4oz)	145g (5oz)	200g (7oz)	255g (9oz)	315g (11oz)	400g (14oz)	515g (18oz)
Ground mace	pinch	pinch	pinch	pinch	pinch	pinch	pinch
Mixed spice	¼tsp	½tsp	½tsp	¾tsp	1tsp	1¼tsp	1½tsp
Ground nutmeg	pinch	pinch	¼tsp	¼tsp	½tsp	½tsp	¾tsp
Baking temperature	----150°C (300°F) or Gas Mark 2---			-----------140°C (275°F) or Gas Mark 1-----------			
Approximate baking time	1¾hrs	2hrs	2½hrs	3hrs	3½hrs	4½hrs	6hrs

BAKING TEST Bring the cake forward from the oven at the end of the recommended baking time so that it can be tested. Insert a stainless steel skewer into the centre of the cake and slowly withdraw it. If the cake is sufficiently baked, the skewer will come out as clean as it went in. Continue baking at the same temperature if the cake mixture clings to the skewer. Test in the same way every ten minutes until the skewer is clean when withdrawn from the cake.

STORAGE Remove the cake carefully from the tin when it is cold and then take off the greaseproof paper. Wrap the cake in waxed paper and leave in a cupboard for at least three weeks.

PORTIONS To estimate the number of portions that can be cut from a finished cake, add up the total weight of all the cake ingredients, almond paste, sugarpaste and/or royal icing. As the average slice of a finished cake weighs approximately 60g (2oz), simply divide the total weight accordingly to calculate the number of portions.

See Hints and Tips on page 12

INGREDIENTS

225g sultanas (8oz)
225g currants (8oz)
225g raisins (8oz)
85g candied peel (3oz)
85g glacé cherries (3oz)
1 lemon
1tbsp rum/brandy
1tbsp black treacle
225g soft (tub) margarine (8oz)
225g soft light brown sugar (8oz)
4 eggs, size 3
60g ground almonds (2oz)
255g self raising flour (9oz)
Pinch of ground mace
¾tsp mixed spice
¼tsp ground nutmeg

EQUIPMENT

20.5cm square cake tin (8in)
OR
23cm round cake tin (9in)
Greaseproof paper
Mixing bowl
Beater
Sieve
Mixing spoon
Skewer

PREPARATION of INGREDIENTS

Weigh all the ingredients separately. Chop cherries in half and carefully clean and remove stalks from all the fruit. Grate the lemon and then mix all the fruit together with rum. Sift the flour, nutmeg, spice and mace together three times. For better results leave overnight in a warm place 18°C (65°F).

PREPARATION of the CAKE TIN

Cut out a length of greasproof paper deeper than the cake tin (enough to cover inside) and then cut along bottom edges at 2.5cm (1in) intervals. Cut a circle or square as required for the base of the tin.
Brush the inside of the tin with soft margarine. Then cover the side with greaseproof paper and place the base into the bottom of the tin. Finally brush the greaseproof paper with margarine.

BAKING

Bake in a pre-heated oven at 140°C (275°F) or Gas mark 1 for approximately 2½ to 3hrs.

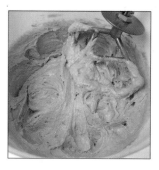

1 Prepare the tin, fruit and other ingredients as described above. Pre-heat the oven. Place all ingredients, except the fruit, into a mixing bowl. Beat together for 2-3 minutes.

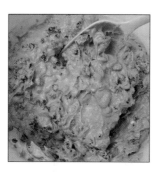

2 Using a spoon, blend in the fruit until well mixed. Place mixture into the tin, level the top and bake.

3 After recommended baking time follow baking test instructions. When baked, leave in the tin until cold. See instructions for storage.

WEDDING CAKE

For hexagonal, octagonal or petal shaped wedding cakes use recipe for the equivalent round cake. Example, for 20.5cm (8in) heart shape use ingredients for 20.5cm (8in) round cake.

Square tin	12.5cm (5in)	15cm (6in)	18cm (7in)	20.5cm (8in)	23cm (9in)	25.5cm (10in)	28cm (11in)
OR							
Round tin	15cm (6in)	18cm (7in)	20.5cm (8in)	23cm (9in)	25.5cm (10in)	28cm (11in)	30.5cm (12in)
Sultanas	170g (6oz)	255g (9oz)	340g (12oz)	425g (15oz)	515g (18oz)	600g (21oz)	680g (24oz)
Currants	170g (6oz)	255g (9oz)	340g (12oz)	425g (15oz)	515g (18oz)	600g (21oz)	680g (24oz)
Raisins	60g (2oz)	85g (3oz)	115g (4oz)	145g (5oz)	170g (6oz)	200g (7oz)	225g (8oz)
Candied peel	30g (1oz)	30g (1oz)	60g (2oz)	85g (3oz)	115g (4oz)	145g (5oz)	200g (7oz)
Glacé cherries	60g (2oz)	60g (2oz)	85g (3oz)	115g (4oz)	170g (6oz)	225g (8oz)	285g (10oz)
Lemon rind (lemons)	½	½	1	1	1	1½	2
Rum/Brandy	1tbsp	1tbsp	1tbsp	1½tbsp	2tbsp	2½tbsp	3tbsp
Butter	115g (4oz)	170g (6oz)	225g (8oz)	285g (10oz)	340g (12oz)	400g (14oz)	450g (1lb)
Dark brown soft sugar	115g (4oz)	170g (6oz)	225g (8oz)	285g (10oz)	340g (12oz)	400g (14oz)	450g (1lb)
Eggs, size 2	1½	2½	4	4½	6	7	8
Ground almonds	30g (1oz)	60g (2oz)	85g (3oz)	85g (3oz)	115g (4oz)	145g (5oz)	200g (7oz)
Plain flour, sifted	115g (4oz)	170g (6oz)	225g (8oz)	285g (10oz)	340g (12oz)	400g (14oz)	450g (1lb)
Ground mace	small pinch	small pinch	medium pinch	medium pinch	large pinch	large pinch	large pinch
Mixed spice	¼tsp	½tsp	¾tsp	1tsp	1¼tsp	1½tsp	1¾tsp
Ground nutmeg	pinch	pinch	¼tsp	½tsp	½tsp	¾tsp	1tsp
Black treacle	½tbsp	½tbsp	1tbsp	1tbsp	1½tbsp	1½tbsp	2tbsp
Baking temperature				140°C (275°F) or Gas Mark 1			
Approximate baking time	2½hrs	3hrs	3½hrs	4hrs	5hrs	6hrs	7½hrs

HINTS AND TIPS

Always line the inside of the cake tin carefully to prevent a mis-shaped cake.

Add egg slowly to batter otherwise it will curdle and result in a poor texture, volume, crumb structure and keeping quality.

Beat in a little of the flour if the batter starts to curdle.

Stir the flour thoroughly into the batter before adding the fruit but be careful not to overmix as this will toughen the batter.

Flour is best added with a wooden spoon.

Batter that has been overbeaten will not support the fruit adequately, causing the fruit to sink during baking.

Always make sure that fruit is clean and is as dry as possible. Do not overwash the fruit.

The cake mixture may be left for up to 24 hours in the tin before baking.

Never bake a cake in a brand new shiny tin. (Remove the shine by placing tin in a hot oven.)

Be careful not to bake in an oven that is too hot. It will produce a cake that has a cracked, crusted top and an uncooked centre. It will also be dark in colour and have bitter tasting, burnt fruit around its crust.

An oven which is too cool produces a pale cake with uncooked fruit and a very thick crust. The cake will go dry and will not keep.

A cake that has been baked at the correct temperature yet sinks in the middle is caused by too much liquid, sugar, fat, or baking powder in the mixture.

The following may result in a cake that is too crumbly: curdled batter, overbeating the fat, sugar and eggs, undermixing the flour and fruit into the batter, insufficient sugar.

WEDDING CAKE

Fruit cake is the traditional medium for wedding cakes as it has excellent keeping properties. When making a fruit cake, timing is important, as it needs at least three weeks to mature.

BAKING TEST At the end of the recommended baking time, bring the cake forward from the oven so that it can be tested.

Insert a stainless steel skewer into the centre of the cake and slowly withdraw it. The cake has been sufficiently baked if the skewer comes out as cleanly as it went in. If the cake mixture clings to the skewer, remove the skewer and continue baking at the same temperature. Test in the same manner every 10 minutes until the skewer is clean when withdrawn from the cake.

SOAKING MIXTURE Equal quantities of glycerin mixed with rum, sherry or any spirits of your choice. The recommended amount of mixture when soaking the cake is 15ml per 450g of cake (1 full tablespoon per 1lb of cake).

STORAGE Carefully remove the cake from the tin when it is cold and then remove the greaseproof paper. Wrap the cake in waxed paper and leave in a cupboard for at least three weeks to mature.

PORTIONS To estimate the number that may be cut from a finished cake simply add up the total weight of all the cake ingredients, almond paste, sugarpaste and/or royal icing. An average slice of a finished cake normally weighs approximately 60g (2oz). Simply divide the total weight by 60g (2oz) to calculate the number of portions.

1 Using table as a guide weigh the ingredients into separate containers. Double check the quantities then mix the prepared fruit and rum/brandy together in a bowl. Leave overnight to soak.

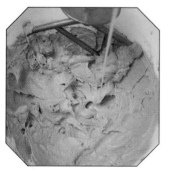

2 Grease the tin with melted butter, line with greaseproof paper then grease the paper. Beat the butter and sugar together until light and fluffy. Then thoroughly beat in the eggs, a little at a time.

3 Stir in the ground almonds, then fold in sifted flour and spices using a spoon or spatula. Do not overmix.

4 Mix in the treacle and soaked fruit until thoroughly blended. Spoon into prepared tin and level, then bake (see baking test).

5 When baked leave in the tin until cold. Remove cake from tin, upturn and remove baking paper. Brush with soaking mixture (see above). Follow storage instructions.

MADEIRA CAKE

For hexagonal, octagonal or petal shaped madeira cakes use recipe for the equivalent round cake. Example, for 20.5cm (8in) heart shape use ingredients for 20.5cm (8in) round cake.

Square tin OR	12.5cm (5in)	15cm (6in)	18cm (7in)	20.5cm (8in)	23cm (9in)	25.5cm (10in)	28cm (11in)
Round tin	15cm (6in)	18cm (7in)	20.5cm (8in)	23cm (9in)	25.5cm (10in)	28cm (11in)	30.5cm (12in)
Butter	60g (2oz)	115g (4oz)	170g (6oz)	225g (8oz)	285g (10oz)	340g (12oz)	400g (14oz)
Caster sugar	60g (2oz)	115g (4oz)	170g (6oz)	225g (8oz)	285g (10oz)	340g (12oz)	400g (14oz)
Eggs, size 2	1	2	3	4	5	6	7
Plain flour	30g (1oz)	60g (2oz)	85g (3oz)	115g (4oz)	145g (5oz)	170g (6oz)	200g (7oz)
Self-raising flour	60g (2oz)	115g (4oz)	170g (6oz)	225g (8oz)	285g (10oz)	340g (12oz)	400g (14oz)
Lemons	¼	½	1	1	1½	1½	2
Baking temperature	------------------------------170°C (325°F) or Gas Mark 3--------------------------------						
Approximate baking time	¾hr	1hr	1¼hrs	1¼hrs	1¼hrs	1½hrs	1½hrs

BAKING TEST Bring the cake forward in the oven at the end of the recommended baking time so that it can be tested. Insert a stainless steel skewer into the centre of the cake and slowly withdraw it. If the cake is sufficiently baked, the skewer will come out of the cake as cleanly as it went in. Continue baking at the same temperature if the cake mixture clings to the skewer. Test every ten minutes until the skewer is clean when withdrawn from the cake.

STORAGE When cold, madeira can be deep frozen for up to six months. Use within three days of baking or defrosting.

PORTIONS A 20.5cm (8in) round madeira cake should serve approximately sixteen portions when decorated.

INGREDIENTS

170g butter (6oz)
170g caster sugar (6oz)
3 eggs, size 2
85g plain flour (3oz)
170g self raising flour (6oz)
1 lemon

EQUIPMENT

18cm square cake tin (7in)
OR
20.5cm round cake tin (8in)
Greaseproof paper
Mixing bowl
Mixing spoon
Spatula

BAKING

Bake in a pre-heated oven at 170℃ (325℉)
or Gas Mark 3 for 1¼hrs.

1 Grease the tin lightly with butter, fully line with greaseproof paper, then grease the paper.

2 Cream the butter and sugar together until light and fluffy.

3 Stir the egg(s) together before beating a little at a time into the creamed mixture (see curdling).

4 Lightly fold the sifted flours into the mixture together with the lemon rind and juice.

5 Place mixture into the tin, and using a spatula, level the top. Bake for recommended time.

6 See baking test instructions. When baked, leave in the tin to cool for 10 minutes before turning out onto a wire rack to cool completely.

ALL-IN-ONE SPONGE CAKE

This sponge is ideal for birthday cakes and cutting into shapes for novelty cakes.
For hexagonal, octagonal or petal shaped sponges use recipe for the equivalent round sponge. Example, for 20.5cm (8in) heart shape use ingredients for 20.5cm (8in) round sponge.

SPONGE TIN SHAPES	SPONGE TIN SIZES					
ROUND	15cm (6in)	18cm (7in)	20.5cm (8in)	23cm (9in)	25.5cm (10in)	28cm (11in)
SQUARE	12.5cm (5in)	15cm (6in)	18cm (7in)	20.5cm (8in)	23cm (9in)	25.5cm (10in)
PUDDING BASIN	450ml (¾pt)	600ml (1pt)	750ml (1¼pt)	900ml (1½pt)	1 litre (1¾pt)	1.2 Litre (2pt)
LOAF TIN		18.5 x 9 x 5cm 450g (1lb)			21.5 x 11 x 6cm 900g (2lb)	
Self-raising flour	45g (1½oz)	60g (2oz)	85g (3oz)	115g (4oz)	170g (6oz)	225g (8oz)
Baking powder	¼tsp	½tsp	¾tsp	1tsp	1¼tsp	2tsp
Soft (tub) margarine	45g (1½oz)	60g (2oz)	85g (3oz)	115g (4oz)	170g (6oz)	225g (8oz)
Caster sugar	45g (1½oz)	60g (2oz)	85g (3oz)	115g (4oz)	170g (6oz)	225g (8oz)
Eggs	1 size 4	1 size 3	1 size 1	2 size 3	3 size 3	4 size 3
Baking temperature	----------------170°C (325°F) or Gas Mark 3----------------------					
Baking time (approximately)	20 mins	25 mins	30 mins	32 mins	35 mins	40 mins

PLEASE NOTE: Baking times for sponges baked in pudding basins and loaf tins may take longer.

BAKING TEST: When the sponge has reached the recommended baking time, open the oven door slowly and, if the sponge is pale in colour, continue baking until light brown. When light brown, run your fingers across the top gently and the sponge should spring back when touched. If not then continue baking and test every few minutes.

STORAGE: When cold the sponge can be deep-frozen for up to six months. Use within three days of baking or defrosting.

PORTIONS: A 20.5cm (8in) round sponge should provide approximately sixteen portions when decorated.

For chocolate flavoured sponges:

For every 115g (4oz) of flour used in the recipe add 2tbsp of cocoa powder dissolved in 2tbsp of hot water, leave to cool then add to the other ingredients in step 3.

For coffee flavoured sponges:

For every 115g (4oz) of flour used in the recipe add 2tsp of instant coffee dissolved in 1tbsp of boiling water, leave to cool then add to the other ingredients in step 3.

For orange or lemon flavoured sponges:

For every 115g (4oz) of flour used in the recipe add the grated rind of one orange or lemon to the other ingredients in step 3.

INGREDIENTS *for Two 20.5cm round sponges (8in) OR Two 18cm square sponges (7in).*

170g self-raising flour (6oz)
1½ teaspoon baking powder
170g soft (tub) margarine (6oz)
170g caster sugar (6oz)
3 eggs, size 3

BAKING

Bake in a pre-heated oven at 170°C (325°F) or Gas Mark 3 for approximately 30 minutes.

EQUIPMENT

Two 20.5cm round sponge tins (8in)
OR two 18cm square sponge tins (7in)
Soft (tub) margarine for greasing
Brush
Greaseproof paper
Mixing bowl
Sieve
Beater
Spatula

1 Grease the tins with soft (tub) margarine, line the bases with greaseproof paper then grease the paper.

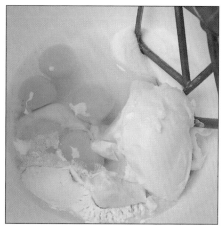

2 Sift the flour and baking powder together twice to ensure a thorough mix. Then place into a mixing bowl with all the other ingredients.

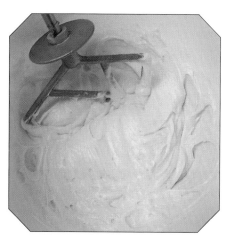

3 Beat mixture for 3-4 minutes until light in colour.

4 Spread the mixture evenly between the two tins. Bake in pre-heated oven (see baking test).

5 When the sponges are baked, leave to cool in the tins for 5 minutes, then carefully turn out onto a wire tray until cold.

6 When cold, sandwich the sponges together with jam and cream then place into a refrigerator for 1 hour before decorating.

SWISS ROLL

INGREDIENTS

85g soft (tub) margarine (3oz)
170g caster sugar (6oz)
3 eggs, size 3
170g self-raising flour, sifted (6oz)

EQUIPMENT

33 x 23cm swiss roll tin (13 x 9in)
Greaseproof paper
Mixing bowl
Beater
Cranked (step) palette knife
Damp tea towel
Caster sugar for dusting

Bake in pre-heated oven at 200°C (400°F) or Gas Mark 6, for 10-12 minutes on the middle shelf.

For chocolate swiss roll dissolve 3 level tbsp of cocoa powder in 3tbsp hot water, leave to cool and add to the above ingredients.

Suggested fillings:
Preserves with a little rum, brandy or liqueur added. Buttercream with the addition of any of the following: melted chocolate, chopped nuts, fresh lemon or orange, chopped glacé fruits.

1 Grease the swiss roll tin with melted margarine, line with greaseproof paper then grease the paper.

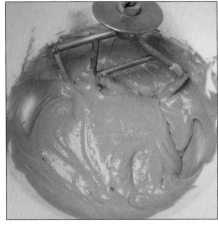

2 Place all the ingredients into a mixing bowl and beat for 2-3 minutes or until well mixed.

3 Spread mixture into the tin evenly. Whilst baking place greaseproof paper, slightly larger than the tin, onto a damp tea-towel.

4 Dredge the paper with caster sugar. When baked, immediately turn out the sponge onto the paper, then remove the baking paper.

5 Leave to cool for a few minutes, spread preserves over the top. (For cream fillings, roll up the sponge, cool, unroll then fill.)

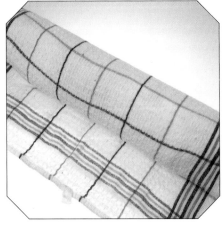

6 Immediately roll up the sponge and keep tightly covered with the damp cloth until cold. Then remove cloth and paper.

BUTTERCREAM and FUDGE ICING

BUTTERCREAM

INGREDIENTS

115g butter, at room temperature
(4oz)
170-225g icing sugar, sifted (6-8oz)
Few drops vanilla extract
1-2tbsp milk

This recipe can be flavoured and
coloured as desired.

FUDGE ICING

INGREDIENTS

200g icing sugar (7oz)
30g golden syrup (1oz)
1½tbsp milk
45g butter (1½oz)

Fudge icing can be used as frosting
or filling, coating cakes and piping.
It can also be frozen and stored in a
refrigerator until required.

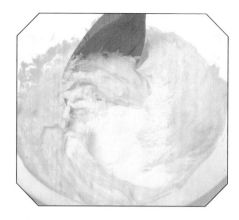

1 For the butter cream: beat the butter until light and fluffy.

2 Beat in the icing sugar, a little at a time, adding the vanilla extract and sufficient milk to give a fairly firm but spreading consistency.

1 For the fudge icing: sift the icing sugar into a bowl. Then put remaining ingredients into a small saucepan and stir over low heat until the butter has melted.

2 Bring to almost boiling then immediately pour the mixture into the icing sugar.

3 Stir until smooth. Follow the suggestions for the various uses of this fudge icing.

ALMOND PASTE

Almond paste is a mixture of uncooked ground almonds, sugar and glucose or eggs. Whereas marzipan is made from cooked ground almonds and sugar. Almond paste can be stored in waxed paper or in a sealed container in a cool, dry place. Do not overmix when making the almond paste. Do not allow the almond paste to come into contact with flour as fermentation may occur.

The almond paste stage in cake decorating is vital in ensuring that smooth layers of icing can be applied later.

Carefully prepare cakes for covering by levelling the top of a domed shape cake or removing the outer edges of a sunken cake. Fill in any imperfections with almond paste and remove any burnt fruit from the surface.

Use icing sugar or caster sugar at all times when rolling out almond paste.

Use boiling apricot purée when fixing almond paste to the cake as this will help prevent mould or fermentation.

When covering a cake, ensure that the layer of almond paste is thick enough to prevent dis-colouring. When covered with almond paste, the cake should have a level top and vertical sides.

After the cake has been covered with almond paste, it should be left to stand in a warm room at about 18°C (65°F) for three to four days. Do not store covered cakes in sealed containers.

USE INGREDIENTS A FOR RECIPE WITH EGGS OR
INGREDIENTS B FOR RECIPE WITHOUT EGGS

INGREDIENTS A

115g caster sugar (4oz)
115g icing sugar (4oz)
225g ground almonds (8oz)
1tsp fresh lemon juice
Few drops of almond essence
1 egg, size 3 or
2 egg yolks, size 3, beaten

INGREDIENTS B

170g icing sugar (6oz)
170g caster sugar (6oz)
340g ground almonds (12oz)
225g glucose syrup, warmed (8oz)

1 For either recipe: mix the dry ingredients together and stir to form an even, crumbly texture.

2 Make a well in the centre, then add the remaining ingredients and mix to a firm but pliable paste.

3 Turn out onto a working surface, dusted lightly with caster or icing sugar, and knead until smooth. Store in a sealed container until required.

COVERING a CAKE with ALMOND PASTE

The following steps are for covering cakes with almond paste ready for coating with royal icing.

For coating cakes with royal icing see page 28.
For covering cakes with sugarpaste see page 30.

1 **For a round cake:** Roll out almond paste using icing or caster sugar for dusting. Brush top of cake with boiling apricot purée. Upturn cake onto the almond paste and then cut around as shown.

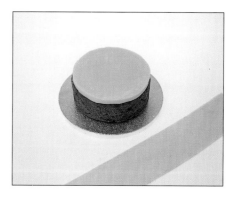

2 Place cake on board. Roll out almond paste into strip that is long and wide enough to cover side of cake in one piece. Spread a thin layer of apricot purée over paste.

3 Fix the almond paste to the side of the cake and trim off the surplus with a sharp knife. Leave to dry for 3 days before coating with royal icing.

4 **For a square cake:** Roll out paste into half the thickness used on the cake top. Cut into 4 equal strips to fit the sides of a square cake. Spread apricot purée on the strips.

5 Fix strips to the sides of the cake. Trim away any surplus cutting towards the centre using a sharp knife. Leave for 3 days before coating with royal icing.

SUGARPASTE

INGREDIENTS

2tbsp cold water
1½ level tsp powdered gelatine
1½tbsp liquid glucose

2tsp glycerin
450g icing sugar, sifted (1lb)

1 Pour the water into a saucepan and sprinkle on the powdered gelatine. Dissolve over low heat. Stir in the glucose and glycerin then remove from the heat.

2 Gradually add and stir in the icing sugar with a spoon, to avoid making a lumpy mixture. When unable to stir anymore icing sugar into mixture, turn out onto table.

3 Mix in the remaining icing sugar using fingers then knead until a pliable smooth paste is formed. Store in a sealed container until required.

MODELLING PASTE

INGREDIENTS

255g icing sugar (9oz)
1 level tbsp gum tragacanth
1 level tsp liquid glucose
8tsp cold water

STORAGE

Store in a refrigerator using a food-approved polythene bag in an airtight container. Always bring to room temperature before use.

1 Thoroughly sift together the icing sugar and gum tragacanth into a mixing bowl

2 Blend the glucose and water together then pour into the dry ingredients and mix well.

3 Knead the mixture by hand until a smooth and pliable paste is formed. To store, see instructions above.

ALBUMEN SOLUTION

INGREDIENTS

15g pure albumen powder (½oz)
85g cold water (3oz)

ROYAL ICING

INGREDIENTS

100g fresh egg whites or
albumen solution (3½oz)
450g icing sugar, sifted (1lb)

If using fresh egg whites,
separate 24 hours before use.

FOR SOFT CUTTING ROYAL ICING

For every 450g (1lb) ready-made
royal icing beat in the following
amounts of glycerin:

1tsp for bottom tier of three
tiered cake.
2tsp for middle tiers.
3tsp for top tiers, single tiers
and general piping.

1 For albumen solution: Pour the
water into a bowl, then stir and
sprinkle in the albumen powder.
Whisk slowly to half-blend in. The
solution will go lumpy. Leave for
1 hour, stirring occasionally.

DO NOT ADD GLYCERIN WHEN MAKING
RUNOUTS, FIGURE PIPING, PIPED FLOWERS
AND LEAVES OR FINE LINE WORK.

2 Pour the solution through a fine
sieve or muslin. It is now ready for
use. Store in a sealed container and
keep in a cool place until required.

1 For making royal icing: Pour the
egg whites or albumen solution
into a bowl. Slowly mix in half the
icing sugar until dissolved.

2 Then slowly mix in the remaining
sugar. Run a spatula around the
inside of the bowl to ensure all the
ingredients are blended together.

3 Thoroughly beat mixture until light
and fluffy. Peaks should be formed
when the spoon or beater is lifted.
Clean down inside then cover
with a damp cloth until required.

COATING CAKES with ROYAL ICING

Royal icing should be made at least 24 hours before use as this allows the strength of the albumen to develop which produces a smooth consistent texture that is ideal for spreading. (Royal icing that has been freshly made is far too fluffy and very difficult to spread evenly.)

The icing should be coated onto an almond paste or marzipan covered cake that has been allowed to dry completely (see page 25).

EQUIPMENT: The most important tool when coating a cake with royal icing is the turntable. It will need occasionally to be lubricated using food approved oil or grease.

For spreading royal icing a stiff, stainless steel palette knife is required. A stainless steel rule serves very well for flattening and levelling the icing on the top surfaces of cakes.

Plastic or stainless steel side scrapers which are not too flexible will produce a smooth finish around the cake-side. Spread fingers across the width of the scraper to ensure an even pressure when rotating the turntable. Remove any marks in the ruler or scraper by rubbing with an emery board. Non-ferrous tools should always be used when using royal icing.

CAKE BOARDS: Always use strong, thick cake boards for fruit cakes to prevent damage when moving.

The cake will be difficult to move once coated therefore it should be positioned exactly on the cake board before coating.

COLOURING ROYAL ICING: If pale coloured royal icing is required, make the first coat white, the second a pale shade of the colour required, and the final coat the actual colour. When strong colours are used, the first coat should be at half strength, the second three quarter strength and the final coat full strength. Always remember to colour enough icing for coating tiers and any other requirements that you might have, as it will be virtually impossible to

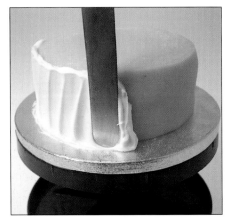

1 Coating a round cake: Carefully position cake on turntable. Spread royal icing around the cake-side using a palette knife.

2 Smooth the icing using a scraper against the cake-side and revolving the turntable one complete turn. Repeat the process until smooth.

3 Using a palette knife, remove any surplus icing from the cake-top and cake board. Then leave to dry for 12 hours.

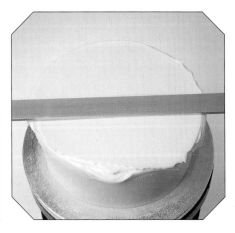

4 Spread icing evenly over cake-top using a palette knife. Level the icing with a steel ruler. Remove surplus icing from edge of cake and leave to dry for 12 hours. Repeat all the steps for two more layers.

match exactly the same colour again. If you make royal icing in a pale shade such as lemon, do not add any blue as this will discolour the icing.

COATING CAKES: When coating cakes with royal icing, there are two techniques which can be used depending on whether sharp or smooth edges are required.

The first method involves starting at the top of the cake and then spreading the icing round and down the sides in one simple operation, flattening and levelling as you work. You will find this method produces a rounded edge.

The second method is a little more time consuming but produces striking results with sharp corners and is particularly suitable for formal designs such as wedding cakes. The second method is the one illustrated below.

Whichever coating method you choose to use, it is normal practice to cover the cake with at least three layers of royal icing. Make the first layer the thickest (which should remove any unevenness in the almond paste cover); the second layer should be about half the thickness of the first layer; while the final layer can be used to create the ideal smooth finish.

Carefully trim each layer of royal icing, when dry, using a sharp knife before applying the next layer. Do not dip the palette knife or ruler in water when applying the icing.

Coloured icing tends to dry to a rather patchy finish if the coatings have been applied unevenly.

DRYING: The coating must be perfectly dry and stable before it can be tiered, which should be at least one week before it is required. Use a simple chart to record dates for covering with almond paste, times for coating and decoration. Drying can take twice as long under adverse conditions such as stormy and humid weather. An airing cupboard is ideal for drying cakes. Avoid storing in humid kitchens and under direct sunlight as these will adversely affect the drying and colour of the cake.

STORAGE: A decorated cake should be stored in a cardboard box. This allows the cake to breathe and the air to circulate which will keep it dry.

TIERING CAKES: *see page 223.*

1 Coating straight-sided cakes: Coat opposite sides of the cake with royal icing and then remove any surplus. Leave to dry for 12 hours. Repeat the procedure for the other 2 sides.

2 With a palette knife spread royal icing evenly over the top of the cake using a paddling motion.

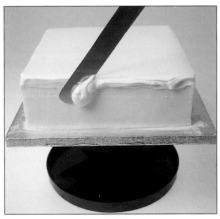

3 Level icing using a ruler until the top of the cake is smooth. Then remove any surplus from edges and leave to dry for 12 hours. Repeat steps 1 to 3 for a further 2 layers.

4 Coating the cake board: Spread royal icing over cake board using a palette knife. Then smooth the icing by holding a scraper and revolving the turntable. Clean the sides and leave for 12 hours.

COVERING CAKES with SUGARPASTE

1 **To cover a round or square sponge cake:** Coat the cake-side and top with a thin layer of buttercream. Chill for 1 hour in the refrigerator.

2 When chilled, roll out the sugarpaste and place over the cake, using the rolling pin.

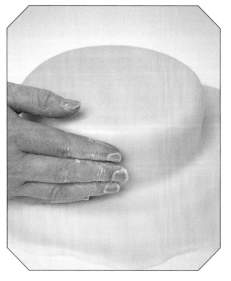

3 Smooth the paste over the top, then down the side, using palm of hand. Trim around the cake-base or board edge. Leave until dry before decorating.

1 **Covering a round or square fruit cake:** Fill-in any imperfections with almond paste. Brush boiling apricot purée over the cake-top and sides.

2 Roll out almond paste, dusting with icing and place over the cake, using the rolling pin. Then press firmly to the cake-top and sides using palm of hand to expel any trapped air. Leave to dry for 24 hours.

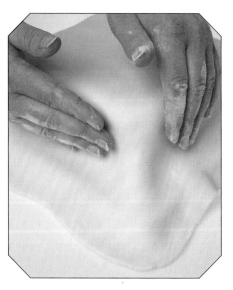

3 Brush the almond paste with cooled boiled water. Roll out sugarpaste, dusting with icing sugar and place over the cake. Smooth to expel any trapped air. Trim paste and leave until dry before decorating.

PIPING TUBES and SHAPES

PIPING TUBES

The diagram shows the icing tube shapes used in this book. Please note that these are Mary Ford tubes, but comparable tubes may be used.

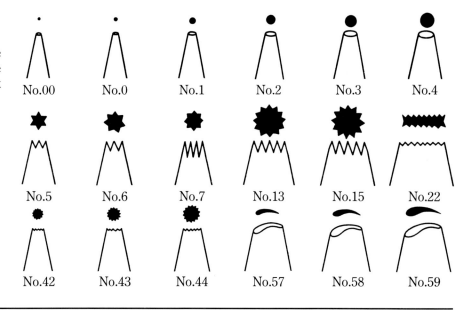

No.00   No.0   No.1   No.2   No.3   No.4

No.5   No.6   No.7   No.13   No.15   No.22

No.42   No.43   No.44   No.57   No.58   No.59

PIPING SHAPES

Shell: Place the piping tube against the surface and press. Continue pressing and start to lift the piping bag. With the piping bag slowly moving upwards, continue pressing until the size required is reached. Stop pressing, move the piping bag down to the surface and pull away to complete the shape.

Rosette: Holding the piping bag upright, move and press in a clockwise direction. On completion of one full turn, stop pressing and draw the piping bag away to complete the shape.

Rope: Holding the piping bag at a low angle, pipe a spring shape along the surface in a clockwise direction. Continue piping until length required, then stop. Pull the piping bag away to complete the shape.

Barrel scroll: Hold the piping bag at a low angle and start to press. Continue piping in a clockwise direction, increasing the size of the circle with each turn. Continue piping in clockwise direction but, from the centre, decrease the size of the circle with each turn. To complete the spiral shell, stop piping and pull bag away in a half-turn.

'C' scroll: Pipe in a clockwise direction, increasing size. Continue piping, reducing size then form the tail using reduced pressure.

'C' line: Holding the piping bag at a slight angle, move and press in an anti-clockwise direction. Release the pressure whilst sliding the piping tube along the surface, to form a tail and complete the shape.

'S' scroll: Hold piping bag at a low angle and start to press. Continue piping in a clockwise direction, increasing the size of each circle to form the body. Continue piping, reducing the size of the circles from the centre. Continue piping and form the tail by reducing the pressure.

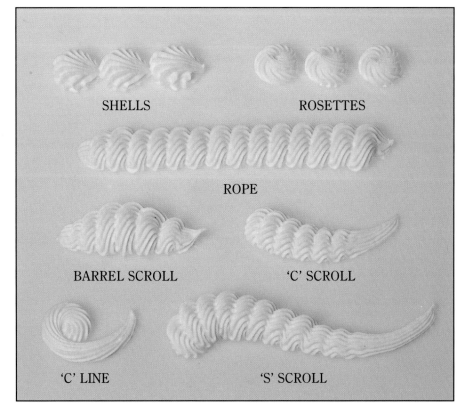

SHELLS   ROSETTES

ROPE

BARREL SCROLL   'C' SCROLL

'C' LINE   'S' SCROLL

TEMPLATES

WESLEY'S CHRISTENING

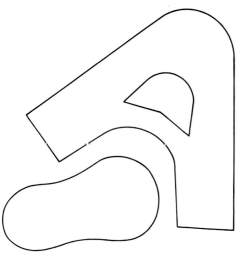

INGREDIENTS

20.5cm square cake (8in)
900g almond paste (2lb)
1.5k sugarpaste (3lb)
115g royal icing (4oz)
Blue food colour

EQUIPMENT and DECORATIONS

25.5cm square cake board (10in)
Piping tubes No.1 and 57
Crimped cutters
Cocktail stick
Narrow ribbons
Ribbon bows
Board edge ribbon

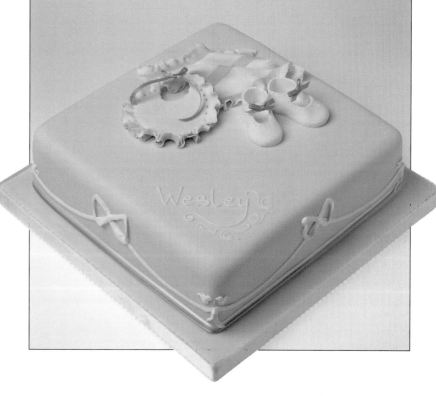

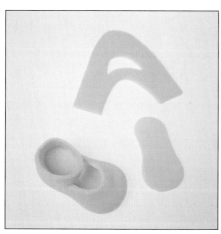

1 Cover the cake and board with sugarpaste. Using the templates as a guide, cut out sugarpaste sole and top. Join together to form bootee. 2 required. Leave to dry for 1 hour.

2 Using crimped cutters, cut two colours of sugarpaste to shape shown. Flute edges then fix together to form a bib.

3 Cut strips of sugarpaste and fix onto sugarpaste cut into an oblong. Roll out then flute the edges to form a shawl. Fix narrow ribbons around the cake-base.

4 Pipe ribbon loops and bows around the cake-sides (No.57) with royal icing. Pipe birds and inscription as shown (No.1). Decorate and fix the sugarpaste items.

Baby Emily

Increase or decrease the size of the template so that the dotted line is equal to the width of the cake being decorated.

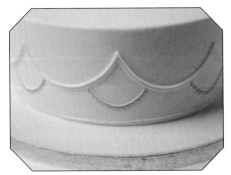

1 Coat the cake and board with royal icing. Outline (No.1) and flood-in the two areas of the runout onto non-stick paper, as shown. Leave until dry.

2 Flood-in the middle section, then pipe the floral design and scalloped edge (No.1). Leave to dry for 24 hours.

3 Divide the cake-side into 8 sections then pipe the curved lines shown (No.2 and 1). Fix the cake board to a larger cake board. Then coat the large board with royal icing.

20.5cm round cake (8in)
680g almond paste (1½lb)
1.5k royal icing (3lb)
Lilac and yellow food colours

33cm round cake board (13in)
28cm round cake board (11in)
Non-stick paper
Piping tubes No.1, 2 and 3
Floral spray of choice
Board edge ribbons

4 Fix the runout to the cake-top. Pipe shells around the inside edge (No.2). Pipe shells around the cake-base (No.3). Pipe filigree around each cake board edge (No.1).

5 Make and fix a floral spray as required.

6 Pipe inscription of choice and decorate with tracery (No.1). Pipe bootees (No.2 and 1).

FLOWER FAIRIES

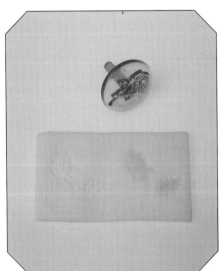

1 Press embosser into sugarpaste and colour with dusting powder to check result. Cover cake and board with sugarpaste. Then continue the design around the board.

2 Cut out a modelling paste crimped circle, brush the edge with dusting powder.

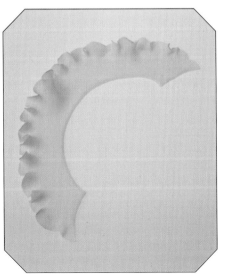

3 Flute the edge, using a cocktail stick, then cut and bend into the curve of the cake-top. 4 pieces required to make the collar. Leave until dry.

INGREDIENTS

20.5cm oval petal shaped cake (8in)
900g almond paste (2lb)
900g sugarpaste (2lb)
450g modelling paste (1lb)
115g royal icing (4oz)
Selection of food colours
Green and pink dusting powders

EQUIPMENT and DECORATIONS

30.5cm oval cake board (12in)
Floral embosser
Cocktail stick
Piping tubes No.1 and 2
Board edge ribbon

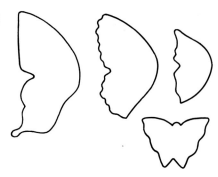

4 Using modelling paste, make and fix a set of frills to the cake-base.

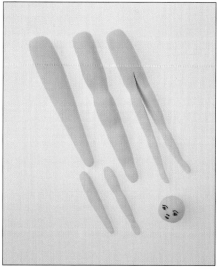

5 Mould modelling paste pieces in the sequence shown, for the body of each fairy.

6 Fix the body pieces together, then dress the fairy as shown. Make a baby in a shawl from modelling paste.

7 Make a fairy in the position shown.

8 Make a fairy in a sitting position as shown. Leave the fairies until dry.

9 Fix the collar pieces to the cake-top. Pipe shells around the edges (No.2). Make and fix sugarpaste flowers. Fix the fairies and baby as required. Pipe the name (No.1).

SWEET DREAMS

INGREDIENTS

25.5cm hexagonal cake (10in)
1.5k almond paste (3lb)
2k sugarpaste (4lb)
225g modelling paste (8oz)
Lilac food colour

EQUIPMENT and DECORATIONS

35.5cm hexagonal cake board (14in)
Fine paint brush
Cocktail stick
Piping tubes No.1 and 2
Floral spray
Board edge ribbon

1 Cover the cake and board with sugarpaste. Pipe shells around the cake-base with royal icing (No.2).

2 Cut out a round disc of sugarpaste, slightly larger than the width of the cake, frill the edge then fix over the cake-top.

3 Using modelling paste, make a shawl, baby and birds. Fix to the cake-top with floral spray. Pipe inscription and tracery around the board edge (No.1).

38

PICTURE FRAME

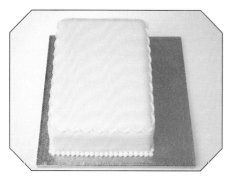

INGREDIENTS

20.5 x 15cm oblong shaped
   sponge (8 x 6in) 2 required
680g sugarpaste (1½lb)
225g royal icing (8oz)

EQUIPMENT and DECORATIONS

25.5cm square board (10in)
Piping tubes No.1 and 42
Crimper
Photograph of choice with
   backing paper

1 Cover the sponge with sugarpaste and immediately crimp the top edge. Fix onto the board and pipe shells around the cake-base with royal icing (No.42).

2 Fix a photograph, backed with silver paper, onto the cake-top and pipe shells around the edge to secure (No.42).

3 Using templates on page 32, cut out and fix sugarpaste figures and hearts. Pipe inscription and tracery (No.1).

1 Roll out together white and small pieces of black sugarpaste to cover one small sponge cake. Then cover the other cakes in the colours shown above in the main picture.

2 Mould sugarpaste to form the various parts shown for the face of the dog.

3 Fix the face pieces to the side of the cake as shown.

INGREDIENTS

6.5cm round sponge (2½in) 6 required
1.5k sugarpaste (3lb)
Assorted food colours
Rice paper

EQUIPMENT

7.5cm cake card (3in) 6 required

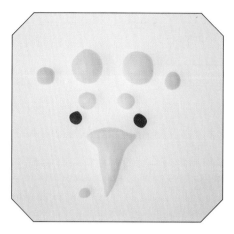

4 Mould and fix the sugarpaste parts shown to form the mouse cake. Then cut and fix strips of rice paper for the whiskers. Fix to the cake as shown in the main picture.

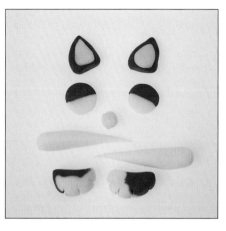

5 Mould the various sugarpaste parts for the kitten.

6 Fix the pieces to the cake then roll out and fix a tail.

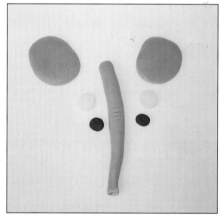

7 Mould and fix the various sugarpaste parts for the elephant. Fix to the cake as shown in the main picture.

8 Mould the various sugarpaste parts for the rabbit.

9 Fix the parts as shown then cut and fix strips of rice paper for the whiskers.

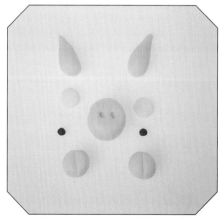

10 Mould and fix the various sugarpaste parts for the pig. Fix to the cake as shown in the main picture.

Nut Mobile

INGREDIENTS

Sponge baked in a 1.2Lt pudding
  basin (2pt)
1.5k sugarpaste (3lb)
225g royal icing (8oz)
Assorted food colours

EQUIPMENT and DECORATIONS

28cm round cake board (11in)
Large stiff paint brush
Drinking straw
Piping tube No.1
Piece of map
Long candle
Board edge ribbon

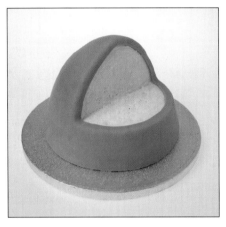

1 Cut the sponge to the shape shown. Cover the outside with sugarpaste and place onto the board.

2 Cover the cut surface with darker coloured sugarpaste then, using a wide stiff paint brush, brush the whole surface with colouring to create streaks.

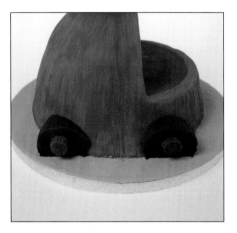

3 Make and fix sugarpaste wheels then stipple the board with royal icing.

4 Mould and cut sugarpaste to shape shown for the squirrel. 2 required.

5 Bend each head down and the arms out. Form the ears and indent for eyes.

6 Brush royal icing over the squirrels to create fur effect.

Happy Birthday

4 YRS

7 Make and fix tails, then fix the bodies. Brush with colouring to finish the squirrels as shown.

8 Cut out and fix sugarpaste number plate, driving wheel and head lights. Fix the map. Pipe age of child with royal icing (No.1).

9 Cut and fix rear number plate and lights from sugarpaste. Use plastic straws for the exhaust pipes and a long candle for the aerial.

ORANGE TREE

INGREDIENTS

25.5cm petal shaped
  sponge (10in) 2 required
7.5cm square sponge (3in)
  2 required
1.5k sugarpaste (3lb)
225g royal icing (8oz)
Assorted food colours

EQUIPMENT and DECORATIONS

35.5cm round cake board (14in)
Piping tubes No.1 and 2
Leaf cutter
Grater
Assorted cake figures
Board edge ribbon

1 Cut one petal off the petal shaped
sponges and cover with sugarpaste.
Then cover the square sponges
with sugarpaste. Fix to the board
then stipple the board with royal
icing as shown.

2 Cut out sugarpaste circles, mark
with the grater and fix to the tree
with sugarpaste leaves. Decorate
as shown (No.1) with royal icing.

3 Decorate the trunk with sugarpaste
eyes, nose and mouth. Decorate
the board as required.

SPACE ROCKETS

INGREDIENTS

20.5cm hexagonal cake (8in)
900g almond paste (2lb)
680g royal icing (1½lb)
225g sugarpaste (8oz)
Assorted food colours

EQUIPMENT and DECORATIONS

28cm hexagonal cake board (11in)
Large paint brush
Piping tube No.1
Star shaped cutter
Assorted space figures
Board edge ribbon

1 Coat the cake and board with royal icing. When dry, stipple the icing with colouring, using a large paint brush.

2 Cut out various types of space rocket from sugarpaste. Leave to dry, then pipe lines and words with royal icing (No.1).

3 Fix the rockets to the cake, then cut out and fix sugarpaste stars and rocks. Pipe inscription of choice (No.1). Fix assorted space figures around the board.

SHOE BOX MICE

1 Glue the covering to the board. Layer the sponges together then cut a slice off the top. Cover the sides with sugarpaste to form the shoe box. Roll out sugarpaste thinly and place into the box as shown.

2 Place the sponge lid onto a thin board and cover with sugarpaste. Pipe the lines and filigree with royal icing (No.2 and 1).

3 Pipe the inscription and decorate with tracery (No.1). Leave to dry.

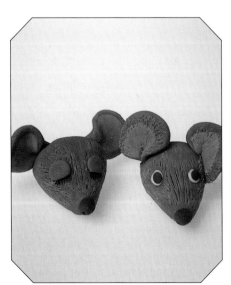

4 Using sugarpaste, mould the mice heads.

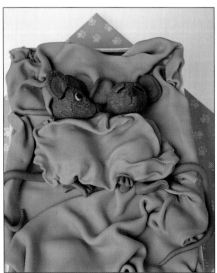

5 Place the heads onto the cake-top, mould and fix the bodies, feet and tails. Cover with thinly rolled sugarpaste as shown.

6 Cut out and fix a sugarpaste shoe to the front of the box. Decorate with piped royal icing as required (No.1).

INGREDIENTS

20.5 x 15cm oblong shaped
  sponge (8 x 6in) 2 required
1.5k sugarpaste (3lb)
115g royal icing (4oz)
Assorted food colours

EQUIPMENT and DECORATIONS

28cm square cake board (11in)
Decorative board covering
20.5 x 15cm oblong shape cake
  card (8 x 6in) 2 required
Piping tubes No.1 and 2

PENGUINS

INGREDIENTS

20.5cm round sponge (8in)   225g royal icing (8oz)
680g sugarpaste (1½lb)   Assorted food colours

EQUIPMENT and DECORATIONS

30.5 round cake board (12in)
Board edge ribbon

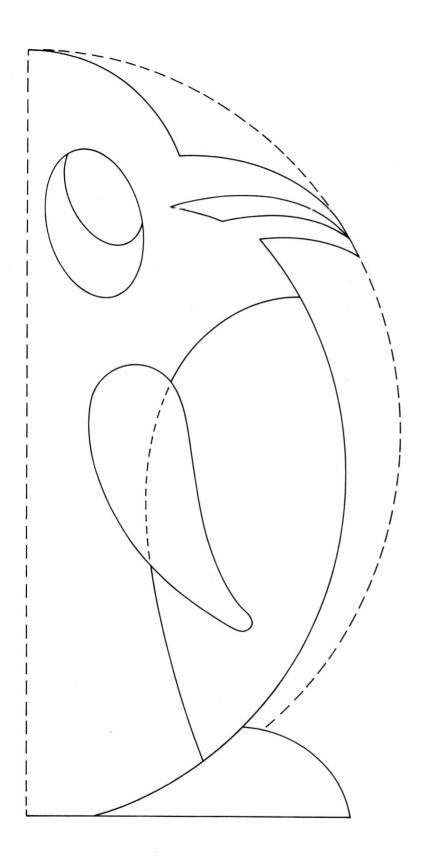

1 Partly cover the board with sugarpaste for the sky, then spread royal icing onto the remaining surface. Lightly stipple icing to form clouds. Leave to dry for 24 hours.

2 Using the template as a guide, cut out the sponge cake then cover with sugarpaste.

3 Cut out and fix the other sugarpaste pieces to complete each penguin. Fix the cakes to the coated board.

TRAIN

1 Cover the oblong sponge with sugarpaste for the base.

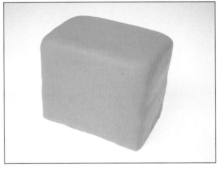

2 Layer together the small sponges and cover with sugarpaste, for the cabin.

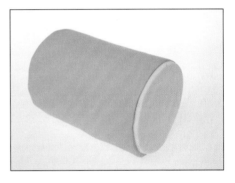

3 Cover the swiss roll with sugarpaste for the engine.

4 Pipe the face onto the front of the engine with royal icing (No.2). Make and fix a sugarpaste nose.

5 Cut and fix a length of sugarpaste down the centre of the board, then stipple royal icing on each side.

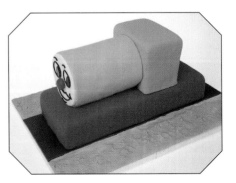

6 Fix all the sections together to form the train.

INGREDIENTS

28 x 10cm oblong shaped
  sponge (11 x 4 in)
10 x 7.5cm oblong shaped
  sponge (4 x 3in) 2 required

Swiss roll
680g sugarpaste (1½lb)
225g royal icing (8oz)
Assorted food colours

EQUIPMENT and DECORATIONS

35.5 x 25.5cm oblong cake board
  (14 x 10in)
Piping tubes No.1, 2 and 4
Round cutters
Candles and candleholders
Board edge ribbon

7 Cut out and fix sugarpaste windows and wheels, then mould and fix the funnels. Pipe the track lines (No.4).

8 Cut and fix sugarpaste buffers to the front and back.

9 Pipe inscription of choice (No.1). Fix candles as required and ribbon around the board.

BABY DINOSAUR

Sponge baked in a 1.2Lt pudding
  basin (2pt)
1.5k sugarpaste (3lb)
450g royal icing (1lb)
Assorted food colours

30.5cm oval cake board (12in)
Expanded drinking straw
Round cutter
Piping tubes No.1 and 2
Numeral
Board edge ribbon

1 Turn the cake upside-down. Trim the base then cover with sugarpaste. Fix to the cake board then stipple the board with royal icing. Leave until dry.

2 Mould and fix the sugarpaste feet, toes and tail.

3 Cut and fix a sugarpaste bib. Stuff the straw with sugarpaste using plastic dowelling. Mould a sugarpaste head, insert the straw, then insert the straw into the body.

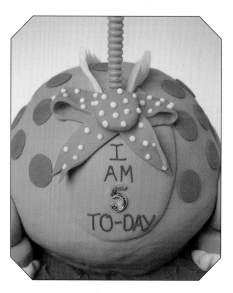

4 Cut out and fix two rows of sugarpaste bones.

5 Cut out and fix sugarpaste spots.

6 Make and fix a sugarpaste bow. Fix the numeral. Pipe inscription (No.1) then dots onto the bow tie with royal icing (No.2).

1 Glue the covering to the board. Cover the sponge with sugarpaste, fix to the cake card then fix to the covered board.

2 Using the template as a guide, cut out the sugarpaste beak, fold in half and fix to the cake-base. Raise the top beak, support if necessary.

3 Cut out and fix sugarpaste eyes. Pipe inscription with royal icing (No.1). Decorate the duck with a party hat and whistle.

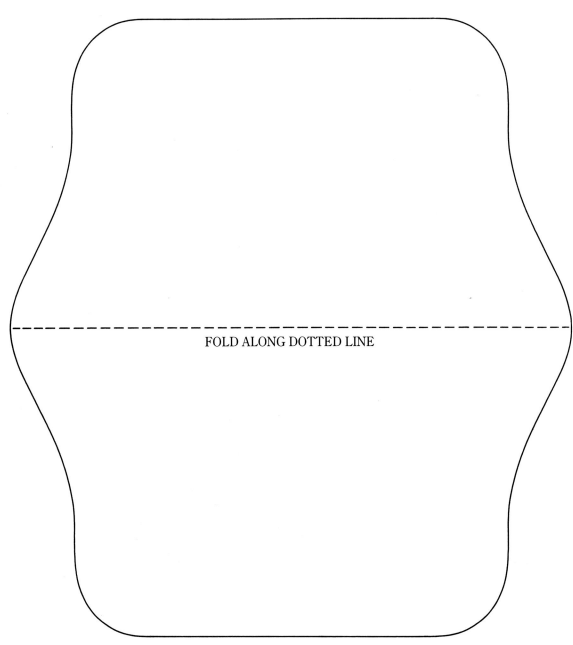

FOLD ALONG DOTTED LINE

QUACKERS

INGREDIENTS

Cake baked in a 1.2Lt pudding
  basin (2pt)
900g sugar paste (2lb)
115g royal icing (4oz)
Assorted food colours

EQUIPMENT and DECORATIONS

30.5cm oval cake board (12in)
Round cake card to fit bottom of sponge
Piping tube No.1
Decorative board covering
Party hat and whistle
Board edge ribbon

BUS RIDE

1 Cut the sponge in half, join together in upright position. Trim the front top and back to shape the bus.

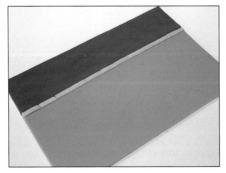

2 Coat the sponge with buttercream and place into refrigerator for 20 minutes. Cover the board with sugarpaste to form the pavement and road.

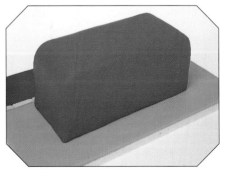

3 Cover the bus with sugarpaste and place onto the road.

20.5cm square sponge (8in)
900g sugarpaste (2lb)
115g royal icing (4oz)
Assorted food colours

30.5 x 20.5cm oblong cake
   board (12 x 8in)
Piping tube No.1

Drinking straw
Candles and candleholders
Board edge ribbon

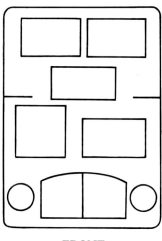

FRONT

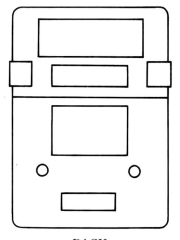

BACK

4 Cut out and fix sugarpaste side
windows, panels, door and wheels.
Pipe the lines and message, with
royal icing (No.1).

5 Cut out and fix front windows,
panel, radiator grill and lights. Pipe
the appropriate bus number (No.1).

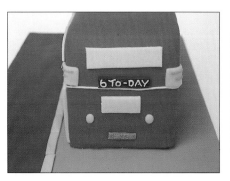

6 Cut out and fix rear windows, lights
and plates. Pipe the lines and
message (No.1).

7 Make and fix a bus stop. Pipe
message (No.1). Fix candles and
ribbon around the board.

STEGOSAURUS

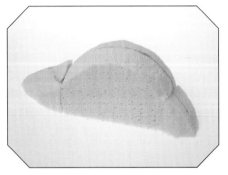

1 Using the template as a guide, cut two sponges and fix together with buttercream to form the shape shown. Coat with buttercream then place in refrigerator to chill.

2 Coat the cake board with mottled royal icing, using a large palette knife. Leave until dry.

3 Cover the sponge with sugarpaste and fix to the board.

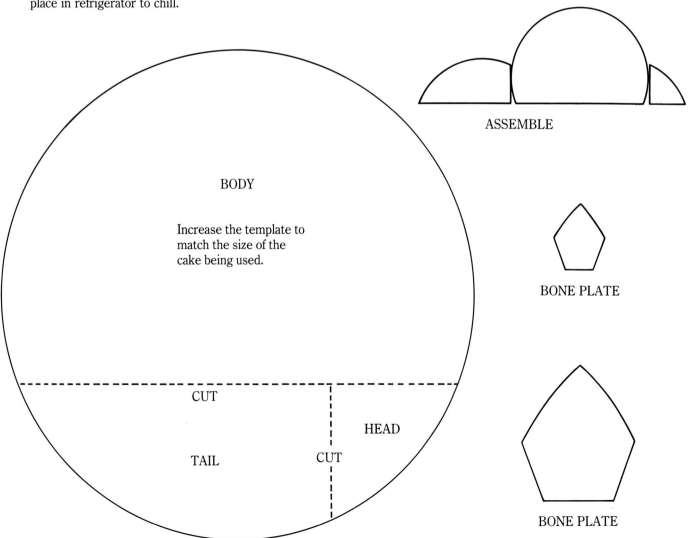

BODY

Increase the template to match the size of the cake being used.

CUT

TAIL   CUT   HEAD

ASSEMBLE

BONE PLATE

BONE PLATE

20.5cm round sponge (8in) 2 required
680g sugarpaste (1½lb)
225g modelling paste (8oz)
225g royal icing (8oz)
Assorted food colours

35.5cm oval cake board (14in)
Paint brush
Piping tubes No.1 and 3
Small sponge
Board edge ribbon

4 Mould and fix sugarpaste legs. Pipe the toes with royal icing (No.3) then the eyes and mouth (No.1).

5 Make and fix the top bone plates and four spikes on the tail, with modelling paste.

6 Brush colouring over the body using a small sponge. Make a modelling paste plaque (see page 32) and pipe inscription of choice (No.1).

CLOWN

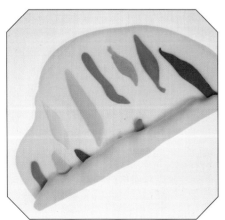

1 Roll out some sugarpaste then place coloured pieces over the surface. Roll up and roll out to form a marbled pattern. Fix onto the cake board and trim.

2 Leave to dry for two hours then cover the sponge with sugarpaste and fix onto the board, in the position shown. Fix the ribbon around the cake-base.

3 Mould the clown's shoes from sugarpaste. Cut out a variety of coloured sugarpaste discs with the crimped cutter, then flute edges with the end of a paintbrush.

INGREDIENTS

20.5cm square sponge (8in)
1.5k sugarpaste (3lb)
Spaghetti strands
Assorted food colours

EQUIPMENT and DECORATIONS

28cm square cake board (11in)
Piping tube No.2
Paint brush
Crimped cutter
Narrow ribbon
Board edge ribbon

4 Fix a length of spaghetti into one shoe and then fix fluted discs with royal icing as shown.

5 Repeat step 4 for second leg and fix to the cake corner. Add discs, made slightly larger, cut and fold to form the body.

6 Make the arms, mould and insert the hands then make and decorate the head.

7 Fix the arms to the body, add more fluted discs for the shoulders then fix on the head. Make and fix hat and flower. Cut out and fix balloons.

8 Pipe the strings and message with royal icing (No.2). Roll strips of sugarpaste over a paintbrush, leave to dry for 1 hour, then peel off to form streamers.

CAULDRON

INGREDIENTS

Sponge baked in a 1.2Lt
  pudding basin (2pt)
900g sugarpaste (2lb)
450g royal icing (1lb)
115g piping jelly (4oz)
Chocolate sticks
Penny mix-up sweets
Assorted food colours

EQUIPMENT and DECORATIONS

30.5cm oval cake board (12in)
18cm round cake board (7in)
Large paint brush
Board edge ribbon

1 Upturn the sponge cake and trim to
the cauldron shape shown. Place
onto the small cake board and
cover with sugarpaste. Press the
handle of a large paintbrush around
the sides to form hammered effect.

2 Coat the large board with royal
icing and make a fire, using
chocolate sticks, sugarpaste and
icing.

3 Upturn the cauldron onto the fire,
remove the cake board and fill with
piping jelly and children's sweets.
Make and fix a sugarpaste handle.

INGREDIENTS

25.5cm round cake (10in)
1.25k almond paste (2½lb)
2k royal icing (4lb)
Assorted food colours

EQUIPMENT and DECORATIONS

35.5cm round cake board (14in)
Piping tubes No.1, 2 and 43
16 drinking straws
16 spaghetti strands
Non-stick paper
Serrated scraper
Piped sugar flowers
Board edge ribbon

1 Coat the cake-top with royal icing and leave until dry. Pipe various colours of royal icing around the cake-side.

2 Immediately spread the icing, using a serrated scraper, in an up and down motion. Spread icing around the board then leave to dry for 24 hours.

3 Outline (No.2) and flood-in onto non-stick paper, a ring of royal icing, slightly smaller than the diameter of the cake. Leave to dry for 24 hours.

64

4 Place a plastic straw onto non-stick paper over a template then pipe-in the horse, covering the straw. Leave to dry for 24 hours. 16 required in various positions.

5 When dry, remove the paper from the horses, upturn then pipe over the top. Leave until dry.

6 Pipe message of choice (No.1) onto the ring runout. Fix flowers with piped leaves (No.1) as required.

7 Decorate the horses in various colours as shown (No.1). Leave until dry.

8 Push 16 strands of spaghetti into the icing in a circle around the cake-top, slightly narrower than the runout ring.

9 Place the straws over the spaghetti and cut to matching height.

10 Pipe shells around the cake-top and base (No.43).

11 Carefully fix the ring to the top of the straws with royal icing. Leave until dry.

12 Pipe loops around the edge of the ring (No.2). Decorate the board with piped flowers and leaves (No.1).

INGREDIENTS

20.5cm round sponge (8in) 2 required
1.5k sugarpaste (3lb)
225g royal icing (8oz)
60g Demerara sugar (2oz)
Assorted food colours

EQUIPMENT and DECORATIONS

38cm round cake board (15in)
Piping tubes No.1 and 2
Board edge ribbon

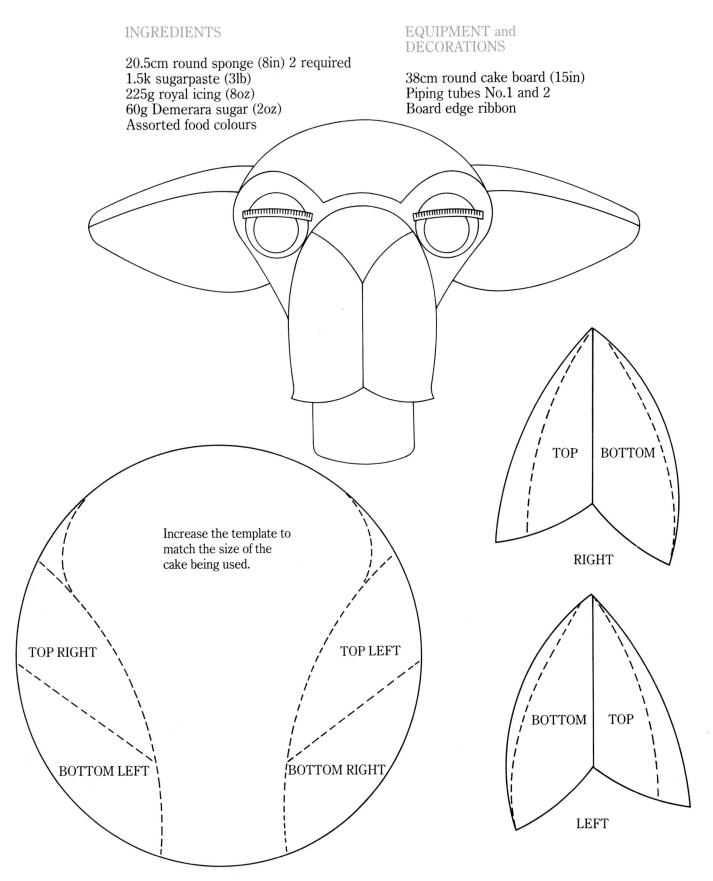

Increase the template to match the size of the cake being used.

TOP | BOTTOM

RIGHT

TOP RIGHT

TOP LEFT

BOTTOM LEFT

BOTTOM RIGHT

BOTTOM | TOP

LEFT

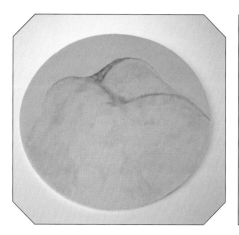

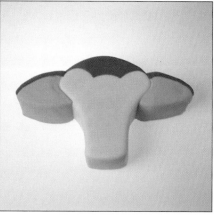

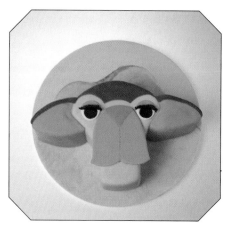

1 Cover the board with two colours of sugarpaste. Stipple the sand colour with royal icing, then sprinkle with demerara sugar to create sand effect. Leave until dry.

2 Using the template as a guide, cut and fix the sponge to shape shown, then cover with sugarpaste to form the camel's head.

3 Fix the head to the cake board. Cut out and fix sugarpaste nose and eyes. Pipe and decorate inscription of choice, with royal icing (No.2 and 1).

MUSICAL FROGS

INGREDIENTS

23cm round cake (9in)
900g almond paste (2lb)
225g royal icing (8oz)
1.75k sugarpaste (3½lb)
1 egg white
Coloured granulated sugar
Assorted food colours

EQUIPMENT and DECORATIONS

28cm round cake board (11in)
Spaghetti strands
Rice paper
Fine paint brush
Board edge ribbon

1 Cover the cake with sugarpaste.
Cut and fix sugarpaste leaves
around the cake-base, then stipple
the board with royal icing.

2 Make a sugarpaste lily leaf. Cut to
shape shown then brush with food
colouring mixed with egg white.
Fix to the cake-top.

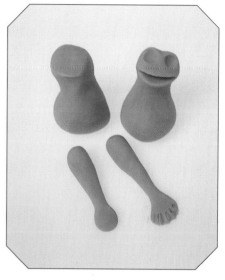

3 Mould sugarpaste to form frog
body and limbs. 5 required.

4 Mould sugarpaste steel drums and
drum sticks. 5 sets required of
differing heights.

5 Fix the frogs together in various
positions. Then mould and fix
sugarpaste eyes. Make and fix a
sugarpaste dragonfly with rice
paper wings.

6 Paint ripples as shown. Make and
fix bullrushes and reeds to the back
of the cake using sugarpaste on
spaghetti, covered with sugar. Fix
the band as required.

MARTIN MARVIL

INGREDIENTS

Sponge baked in a 1.2Lt pudding basin (2pt)
1.25k sugarpaste (2½lb)
Assorted food colours

EQUIPMENT and DECORATIONS

30.5cm oval cake board (12in)
Piping tube No.1
Small piece of ribbon
Board edge ribbon

1 Cut a wedge from the side of the sponge cake and fix it to the top. Spread buttercream over the cake, place in refrigerator to chill.

2 When chilled, smooth the cream then cut out and fix sugarpaste mouth.

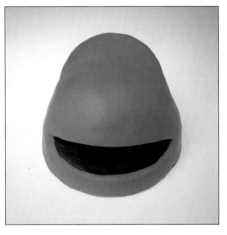

3 Cover the cake with sugarpaste.

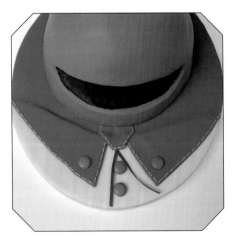

4 Cut out and fix sugarpaste shirt and collar onto the board. Then fix the cake as shown. Pipe stitches with royal icing (No.1). Make and fix sugarpaste buttons.

5 Make and fix sugarpaste eyebrows and then the eyes.

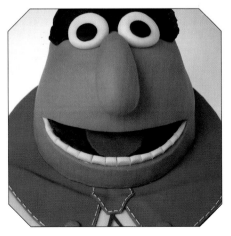

6 Make and fix sugarpaste teeth and tongue. Pipe inscription on the collar (No.1).

TROPICAL FISH

INGREDIENTS

25.5cm petal shaped sponge (10in) 2 required
1.5k sugarpaste (3lb)
115g royal icing (4oz)
Assorted food colours

EQUIPMENT and DECORATIONS

30.5cm petal shaped cake board (12in)
Wide wire sieve
Piping tube No.1
Board edge ribbon

1 Layer, then cut the sponges through the centre at an angle, turn the top slice around and join together. Cover the sponge and board with mottled sugarpaste.

2 Push sugarpaste through a sieve to create sea-anemones and fix a large clump in the centre, with small clumps around the cake.

3 Make and decorate fish as shown. When dry, fix to the cake with sugarpaste rocks. Pipe inscription of choice with royal icing (No.1).

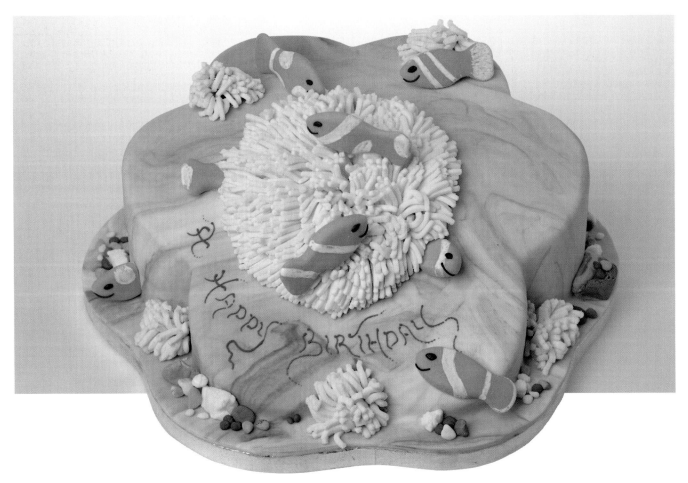

ANIMAL CAPERS

INGREDIENTS

30.5 round sponge (12in) 2 required
1.5k sugarpaste (3lb)
450g royal icing (1lb)
225g piping gel (8oz)
Assorted food colours

EQUIPMENT and DECORATIONS

35.5cm round cake board (14in)
Piping tube No.1
Hundreds and thousands
Candles and candleholders
Board edge ribbon

1 Cover the cake with sugarpaste, place on board then coat the board with royal icing. Using templates as a guide, outline figures onto the cake-top with royal icing (No.1).

73

2 Using coloured piping gel, fill-in the various sections of the seal.

3 Using coloured piping gel, fill-in the various sections of the duck.

4 Using coloured piping gel, fill-in the various sections of the pig.

5 Using coloured piping gel, fill-in the various sections of the rabbit.

6 Using coloured piping gel, fill-in the various sections of the frog.

7 Using coloured piping gel, fill-in the various sections of the dog.

8 Using coloured piping gel, fill-in the various sections of the squirrel.

9 Using coloured piping gel, fill-in the various sections of the elephant.

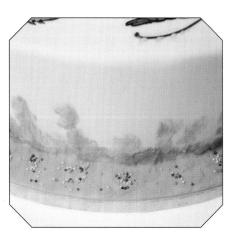

10 Stipple royal icing around the cake-base and board then sprinkle on hundreds and thousands as shown.

PICNIC TIME

INGREDIENTS

20.5cm hexagonal cake (8in)
900g almond paste (2lb)
1.5k royal icing (3lb)
Assorted food colours

EQUIPMENT and DECORATIONS

28cm hexagonal cake board (11in)
Piping tubes No.1, 2 and 42
Non-stick paper
Fine paint brush
Board edge ribbon

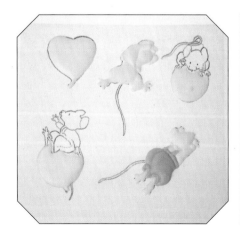
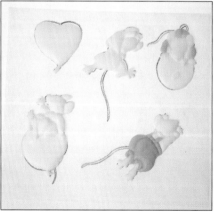
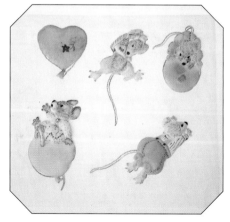

1 Coat the cake and board with royal icing. Using the templates as a guide, pipe-in the areas shown with royal icing onto non-stick paper. Leave to dry for 5 minutes.

2 Pipe-in the further areas as shown. Leave to dry for 24 hours.

3 When dry, paint the pieces in the manner shown.

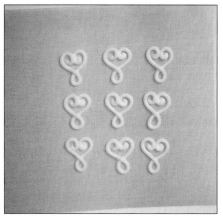

4 Pipe the lace pieces onto non-stick paper (No.2). Leave to dry for 12 hours. Approximately 60 pieces are required.

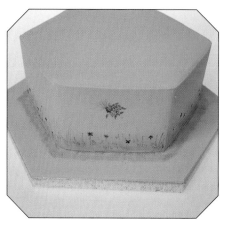

5 Paint the scenery around the cake-sides and base.

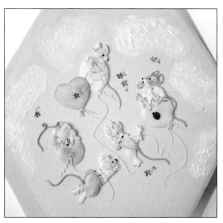

6 Fix the runouts to the cake-top, pipe the tails and balloon strings (No.1). Stipple royal icing to form clouds then paint the flowers as shown.

7 Fix runouts around the cake-sides and decorate.

8 Pipe scrolls around the cake-top edge (No.42) then pipe bulbs as shown (No.2).

9 Fix the lace around the edge of the cake board as shown, then fix the ribbon around the board edge.

Dragon

1 Coat the cake and board in various colours of royal icing. Leave until dry.

2 Pipe flames with royal icing, using cut piping bags without a tube.

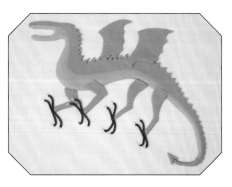

3 Using the template as a guide, cut out and fix a sugarpaste dragon onto the cake-top. Pipe the talons (No.2).

25.5cm oval cake (10in)
900g almond paste (2lb)
900g royal icing (2lb)
225g sugarpaste (8oz)
Assorted food colours

35.5cm petal cake board (14in)
Piping tubes No.1 and 2
Small sponge
Board edge ribbon

 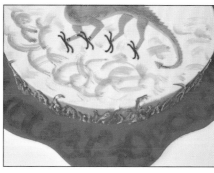 

4 Pipe flames and lines (No.1). Then brush the dragon with colouring using a small sponge.

5 Colour the cake-top and board, using a small sponge.

6 Pipe inscription of choice (No.1). Fix the ribbon around the board edge.

HUMMING BIRD

INGREDIENTS

20.5cm round cake (8in)
680g almond paste (1½ lb)
1.5k sugarpaste (3lb)
340g royal icing (12oz)
Edible gold colour
Assorted food colours

EQUIPMENT and DECORATIONS

28cm round cake board (11in)
Piping tube No.1
Paint brush
Non-stick paper
Cocktail stick
Narrow ribbon
Board edge ribbon

For the brush embroidery piping:

Mix 1tsp of piping gel with 4tbsp
  of royal icing.
Colour as required.

1 Cover the cake and board with sugarpaste. Fix ribbon around the cake-base. Make and fix 3 layers of frill. Pipe shells with royal icing (No.1) along top edge of frill.

Increase the template to match the size of the cake being used.

2 Brush embroider (see glossary) the flower, bud and leaves onto non-stick paper. Leave to dry for 24 hours.

3 Brush embroider the bird onto non-stick paper. Leave to dry for 24 hours.

4 Trace the branch onto the cake-top and brush embroider the areas shown.

5 When dry, fix the flower, bud, bird and leaves as shown.

6 Pipe the inscription with royal icing (No.1). When dry, colour with edible gold. Fix ribbon around the board.

81

FOOTBALL SHIRT

1 Cut and cover the sponge with sugarpaste using the template as a guide.

2 Cut and fix sugarpaste strips as shown.

3 Cut and fix the remaining pieces for the shirt, cup and ball. Decorate with royal icing (No.1).

INGREDIENTS

23cm square sponge (9in)
900g sugarpaste (2lb)
Green, red and black food colours

EQUIPMENT and DECORATIONS

35.5cm round cake board (14in)
Piping tube No.1
Small flower
Narrow ribbon

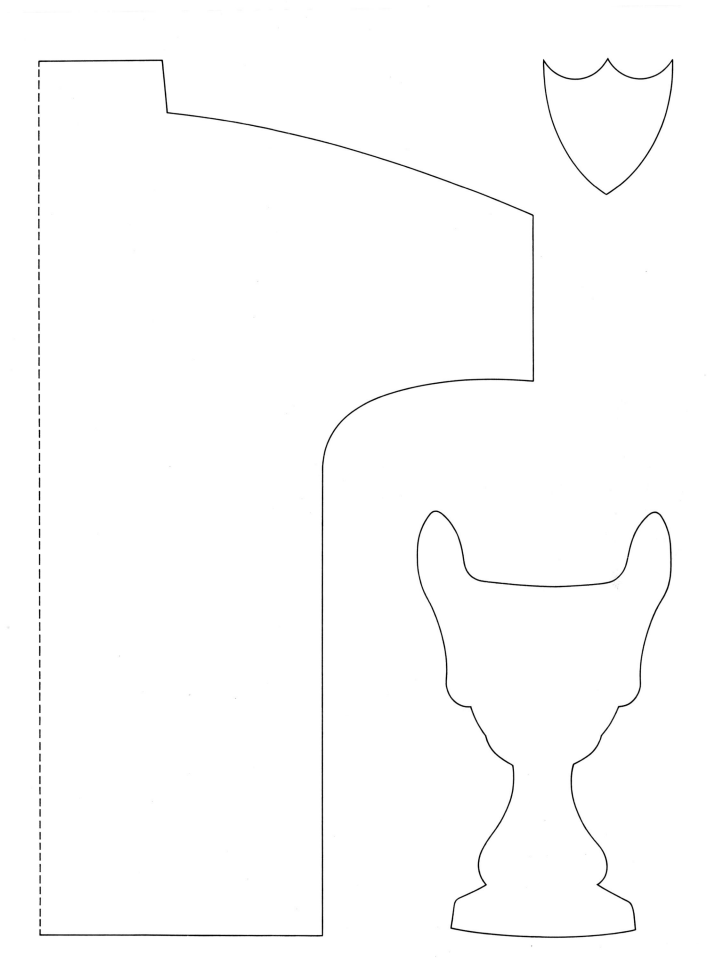

SQUAW PANTS

INGREDIENTS

20.5cm square sponge
  (8in) 2 required
900g sugarpaste (2lb)
Assorted food colours

EQUIPMENT and DECORATIONS

30.5cm round cake board (12in)
Piping tube No.1
Embosser
Fork

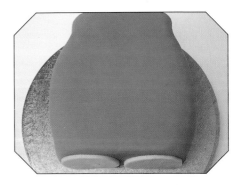

1 Cut and layer the sponges to shape then cover with sugarpaste, as shown.

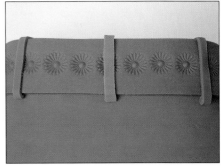

2 Make and fix sugarpaste belt and loops. Press with embosser to form the pattern on the belt.

3 Cut and fix sugarpaste pockets marking with a fork to make stitches, seams and frills. Make and fix a sugarpaste plaque as required. Pipe message with royal icing (No.1).

ROSETTE

INGREDIENTS

20.5cm round cake (8in)
680g almond paste (1½lb)
680g royal icing (1½lb)
450g sugarpaste (1lb)
Assorted food colours

EQUIPMENT and DECORATIONS

28cm round cake board (11in)
Serrated scraper
Piping tubes No.1 and 6
Board edge ribbon

1 Coat the cake and board with royal icing, on the last coat use a serrated scraper around the cake-side. Leave to dry for 24 hours. Pipe shells around the cake-base, with royal icing (No.6).

2 Cut out a sugarpaste circle and, using the end of a cocktail stick, roll back and forth to form a frill around the edge. Make and fix three circles onto the cake-top as shown.

3 Cut out and fix sugarpaste ribbons. Pipe inscription of choice, with royal icing (No.1).

EIGHTEENTH

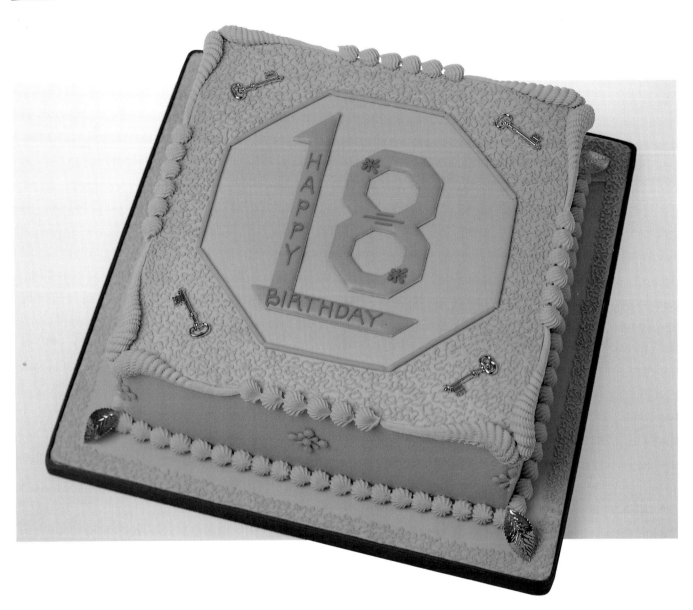

1 Coat the cake and board with royal icing. Using the template as guide outline (No.1) and flood-in the numbers onto non-stick paper. Leave to dry for 24 hours.

2 Cut out a card template and place onto the cake-top. Pipe a line around the template (No.3). Leave to dry for 10 minutes.

3 Remove the template then pipe filigree around the cake-top (No.1).

20.5cm square cake (8in)
900g almond paste (2lb)
900g royal icing (2lb)
Brown and blue food colours

28cm square cake board (11in)
Piping tubes No.1, 3 and 43
Non-stick paper
Card for template
Miniature gold keys
Board edge ribbon

4 Pipe scrolls on each cake-top corner (No.43).

5 Pipe shells between the scrolls, then around the cake-base (No.43). Pipe filigree around the board edge (No.1).

6 Pipe a floral motif on each cake-side and corner (No.2). Decorate and fix the runout numbers (No.1). Fix keys and leaves onto the cake and ribbon around the board.

Coming of Age

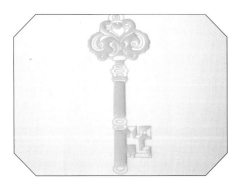

1 Cover the cake and board with sugarpaste. Outline the key with royal icing onto non-stick paper (No.1). Then flood-in the parts of the key as shown. Leave to dry for 15 minutes.

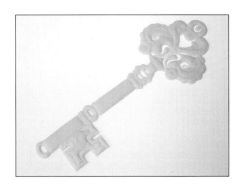

2 Flood-in the remaining areas then leave to dry for 24 hours.

3 Using modelling paste, make a selection of flowers, pulled flowers and buds. Leave to dry for 24 hours.

4 When dry, tape the flowers together with coloured sprigs of dried gypsophilia.

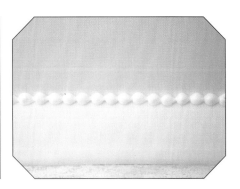

5 Pipe shells along the cake-base, with royal icing (No.2).

30.5 x 18cm oblong shaped
  cake (12 x 7in)
2k almond paste (4lb)
2k sugarpaste (4lb)
450g royal icing (1lb)
225g modelling paste (8oz)
Assorted food colours

35.5 x 25.5cm oblong cake
  board (14 x 10in)
Piping tubes No.1 and 2
Non-stick paper
Gypsophilia (dried)

Tape and wire
Flower holder
Narrow ribbon
Board edge ribbon

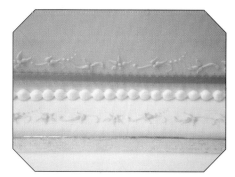

6 Fix a narrow ribbon around the cake-side. Pipe a floral design above the ribbon and on the cake board (No.1).

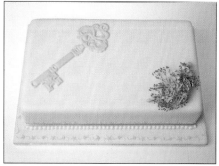

7 Insert a flower holder into the cake-top and place in the spray. Fix the key as shown.

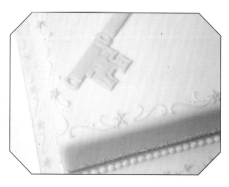

8 Pipe curved lines on the cake-top edge and decorate with piped flowers (No.1). Pipe age and inscription of choice (No.1).

SPORTS DAY

INGREDIENTS

25.5cm hexagonal cake (10in)
1.5k almond paste (3lb)
1.5k sugarpaste (3lb)
450g royal icing (1lb)
Violet and black food colours

EQUIPMENT and DECORATIONS

35.5cm hexagonal cake
  board (14in)
Piping tubes No.1, 2 and 3
Paint brush
Leaves and blossoms
Board edge ribbon

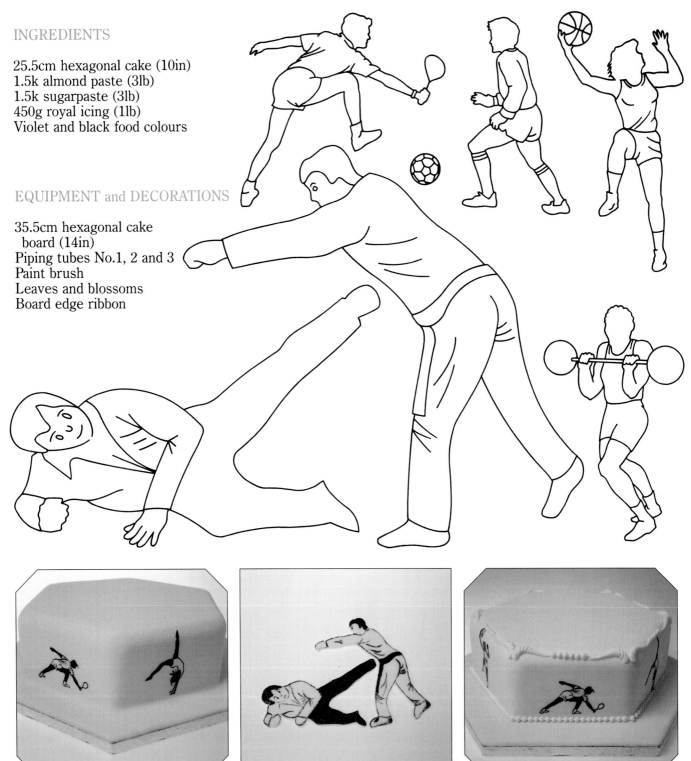

1 Cover the cake and board with sugarpaste, then leave to dry. Trace the templates onto the cake-side and paint with black food colouring.

2 Trace the large figures onto sugarpaste, cut out and paint. Leave to dry.

3 Pipe the scrolls and shells as shown, with royal icing (No.3).

  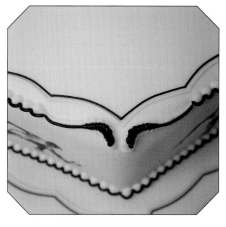

4 Pipe the lines on the cake-top and board (No.2).

5 Overpipe the scrolls then pipe a line over the shells (No.2).

6 Pipe a line beside the No.2 lines (No.1). Fix the cut out figures to the cake-top. Pipe message of choice (No.1). Decorate the cake with blossoms and leaves.

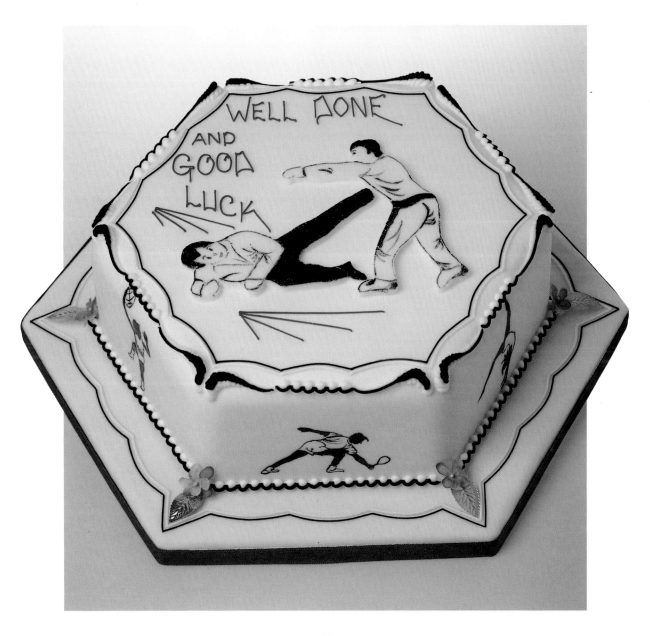

LIFEBUOY

1 Cover the cake and board with mottled sugarpaste.

2 Cut out and fix sugarpaste ring, then four pieces on top, as shown.

3 Cut out and fix sugarpaste sailing boats around the cake-side.

4 Pipe rope lines with royal icing (No.42) as shown, around the cake-side.

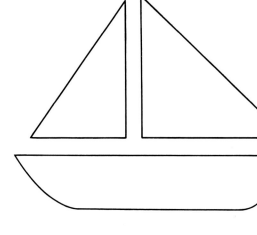

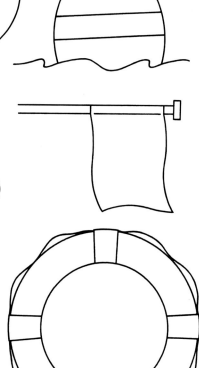

5 Cut out and fix a sugarpaste flag. Pipe inscription of choice (No.1).

25.5cm round cake (10in)
1.25k almond paste (2½lb)
1.5k sugarpaste (3lb)
225g royal icing (8oz)
Assorted food colours

30.5cm round cake board (12in)
Piping tubes No.1 and 42
Board edge ribbon

INGREDIENTS

28cm square cake (11in)
Swiss roll
1.75k almond paste (3½lb)
1.75k royal icing (3½lb)
225g sugarpaste (8oz)
340g modelling paste (12oz)
Assorted food colours

EQUIPMENT and DECORATIONS

38 x 30.5cm oblong cake
  board (15 x 12in)
Piping tube No.1
Label
Board edge ribbon

1 Place the cake onto the board and roughly coat with royal icing, to form the river and bank.

2 Cover the swiss roll with sugarpaste to make a can. Make a modelling paste lid. Leave until dry.

3 When dry, fix a label of choice around the can, then fix the lid as shown.

4 Make and decorate a selection of worms from modelling paste and royal icing.

5 Fix the can and worms to the cake-top. Make a sugarpaste towel then pipe inscription of choice, with royal icing (No.1).

6 Make and fix sugarpaste fish, then pipe the ripples with royal icing.

JUNGLE FUN

INGREDIENTS

23cm round cake (9in)
900g almond paste (2lb)
1.5k sugarpaste (3lb)

225g royal icing (8oz)
Assorted food colours

EQUIPMENT and DECORATIONS

30.5cm round cake board (12in)
Fine paint brush
Board edge ribbon

1 Cover the cake with sugarpaste. Stipple the board and cake-base with royal icing to form grass effect. Make and fix sugarpaste palm trees around the cake-side.

2 Cut and fix sugarpaste palm leaves.

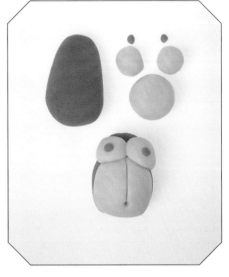

3 Mould the various parts of the ape's body and fix together.

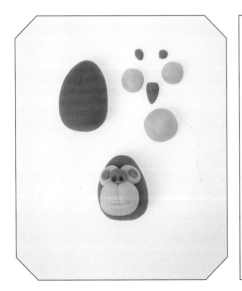

4 Mould the various parts of the ape's head and fix together.

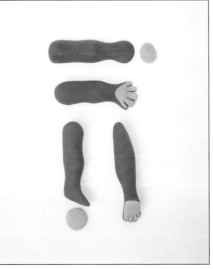

5 Mould the various parts of the ape's limbs and fix to body.

6 Fix all the parts together on the edge of a board, in a sitting position.

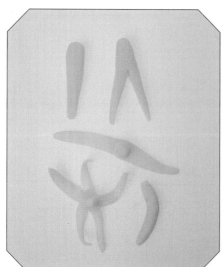

7 Mould and cut a selection of bananas and skins.

8 Colour the banana skins then fix together to spell the message.

9 Fix the ape to the cake-top edge with bananas as shown.

AIR BALLOON

INGREDIENTS

25.5cm oval cake (10in)
1.5k sugarpaste (3lb)
340g royal icing (12oz)
Assorted dusting powders
Assorted food colours

EQUIPMENT and DECORATIONS

35.5cm oval cake board (14in)
Piping tubes No.1, 2 and 42
Board edge ribbon

1 Cover the cake and board with sugarpaste. Cut and fix a sugarpaste balloon, basket and heads. Brush balloon and board with dusting powders.

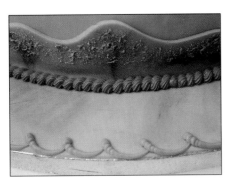

2 Cut and fix a wavy strip of sugarpaste around the cake-side, then colour and stipple with royal icing to form trees. Pipe rope around the cake-base (No.42) and then 'C' scrolls around the board (No.2).

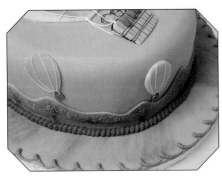

3 Cut and fix small balloons around the cake-side then pipe the lines (No.1). Pipe and decorate inscription (No.1).

FISHING RABBIT

INGREDIENTS

20.5cm oval cake (8in)
680g almond paste (1½lb)
900g royal icing (2lb)
Assorted food colours

EQUIPMENT and DECORATIONS

28cm oval board (11in)
Piping tubes No.1 and 2
Fine paint brush
Non-stick paper
3 cake pillars
Board edge ribbon

 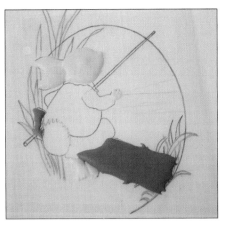 

1 Coat the cake and board with royal icing. Trace the template onto greaseproof paper then cover with non-stick paper. Pipe-in the areas shown, with royal icing. Leave until set.

2 Pipe in the other areas as shown. Leave until set.

3 Pipe-in the other areas as shown. Leave until set.

4 Pipe-in the other areas as shown. Leave until set.

5 Decorate with brushed lines and piping. Pipe and decorate the fish and bread on separate paper. Leave for 24 hours or until dry.

6 Trace the scenery and fishing rod onto the cake-top then paint with liquid and dusting powders.

7 Using the template as a guide, trace the curves onto the cake-side. Pipe shells around the cake-base (No.2). Tilt the cake, then pipe two (No.2) lines then three (No.1) lines to form the bridge as shown.

8 Pipe two (No.2) lines then three (No.1) lines for the higher bridge, at a rising angle as shown. Pipe the suspended vertical lines from under the top bridge to the outside edge of the lower bridge (No.1).

9 Pipe the top vertical lines from the traced line to the outside of the top bridge (No.1). Pipe the dots shown (No.1). Leave until dry.

10 Carefully upturn the cake onto pillars. Pipe loops around the edge and icicle shapes as shown (No.1). Leave until dry then upturn the cake.

11 Fix the runouts to the cake-top, pipe the fishing line (No.1) and decorate as shown.

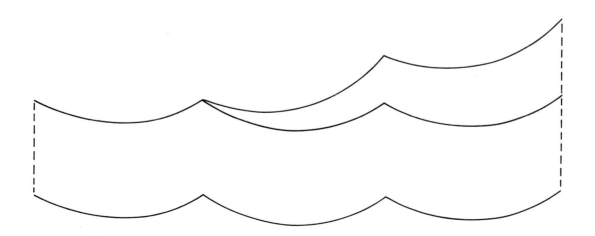

WELCOME HOME

INGREDIENTS

20.5cm square cake (8in)
900g almond paste (2lb)
1.5k sugarpaste (3lb)
115g royal icing (4oz)
Pink dusting powder
Assorted food colours

EQUIPMENT and DECORATIONS

28cm square cake board (11in)
20.5cm square cake card (8in)
Plastic doyley
Soft brush

Serrated scraper
Coarse mesh
Piping tubes No.1 and 2
Board edge ribbon

1 Cover the cake with sugarpaste. When dry, brush dusting powder through a doyley onto the cake to create wallpaper effect.

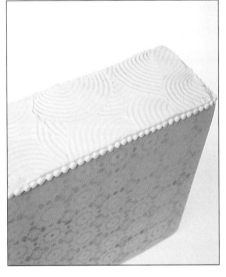

2 Place the cake upright and fix the cake card to the back. Spread royal icing on the cake-top, using a serrated scraper. Pipe shells around the cake-top edge (No.2).

3 Cover the cake board with sugarpaste, place the mesh on top and press with a rolling pin to form carpet effect. Fix the cake in position shown.

4 Make and fix a sugarpaste skirting-board with a cut-out mouse hole.

5 Mould a sugarpaste cat head and paws. Fix to the corner of the board.

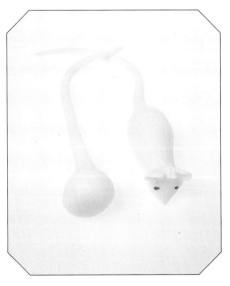

6 Make and fix sugarpaste mice to the hole. Make a sugarpaste plaque then decorate with royal icing (No.1). Fix it to the wall when dry.

102

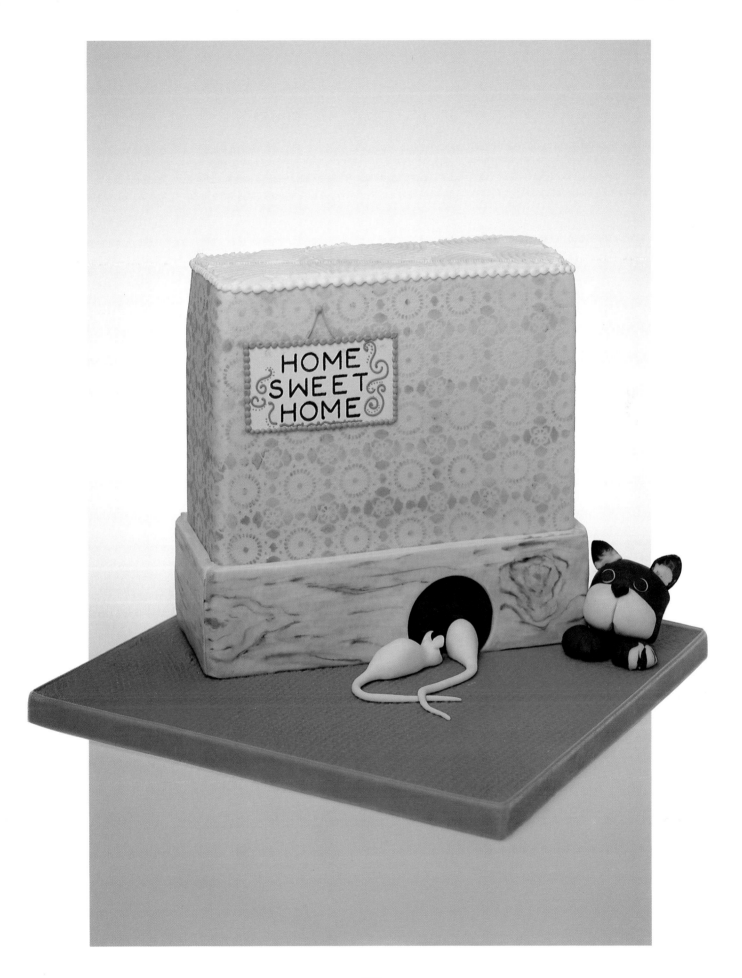

EASTER BUNNY

INGREDIENTS

20.5cm round cake (8in)
680g almond paste (1½lb)
680g sugarpaste (1½lb)

340g royal icing (12oz)
115g piping gel (4oz)
Assorted food colours

EQUIPMENT and DECORATIONS

28cm round cake board (11in)
Piping tube No.1
Assorted sugarpaste flowers
Board edge ribbon

104

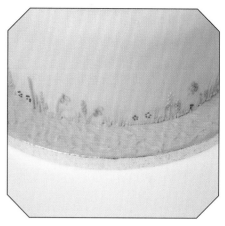

1 Cover the cake with sugarpaste. Using the template as a guide, pipe the bunny and flower with royal icing (No.1).

2 Fill in the sections, using piping gel in various colours.

3 Stipple royal icing around the cake board then pipe the floral design shown (No.1).

4 Pipe inscription of choice (No.1).

5 Pipe the cloud shapes (No.1). Decorate the board with sugarpaste flowers.

MUM'S DELIGHT

INGREDIENTS

20.5cm round cake (8in)
680g almond paste (1½lb)
900g royal icing (2lb)
Assorted food colours

EQUIPMENT and DECORATIONS

28cm round cake board (11in)
Leaf shaped piping bag or
  piping tube

Piping tubes No.1, 2 and 57
Board edge ribbon

1 Coat the cake and board with royal icing. Pipe a selection of sugar flowers, using royal icing, onto non-stick paper (No.57). Leave to dry for 24 hours. Approximately 60 required.

2 Tilt the cake and then using the appropriate templates as a guide, pipe the designs shown (six of each) around the cake-side (No.2 and No.1).

3 Pipe shells around the cake-base (No.2). Then pipe the floral motif around the cake board edge (No.1).

4 Fix the flowers in a circle onto the cake-top.

5 Pipe leaves between the flowers, using a leaf shaped piping tube or bag.

6 Pipe inscription of choice (No.1).

7 Pipe shells around the cake-top edge (No.2) then pipe a line over the shells (No.1).

GARDEN BOOT

INGREDIENTS

2 swiss rolls
1.5k sugarpaste (3lb)
285g almond paste (10oz)
340g royal icing (12oz)
Assorted food colours

EQUIPMENT and DECORATIONS

30.5cm oval cake board (12in)
Food-approved plastic rod
Piping tube No.1
Assorted sugarpaste flowers
Board edge ribbon

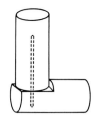

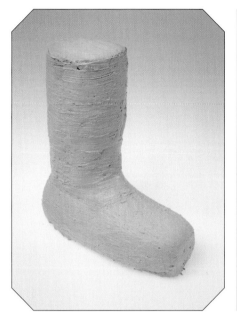

1 Cut and shape swiss rolls to form a boot. Insert the plastic rod for support. Coat with buttercream and chill in refrigerator.

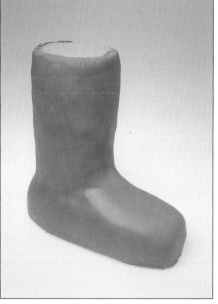

2 When chilled, cover the boot with sugarpaste.

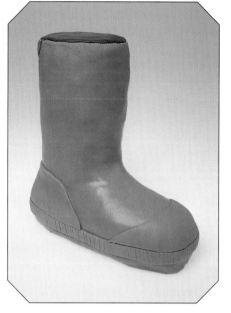

3 Cut out and fix sugarpaste heel, toe, sole and boot top.

4 Place the boot onto the cake board then stipple the remaining surface with royal icing.

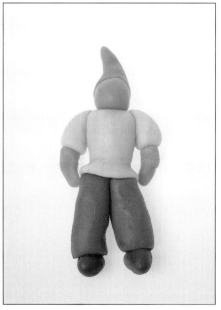

5 Mould and shape a gnome from almond paste.

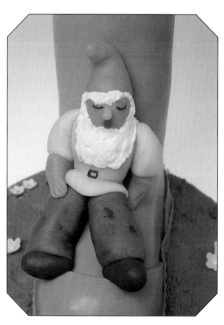

6 Fix the gnome to the boot and decorate with royal icing. Fix sugarpaste flowers and pipe the leaves as required.

TREE SQUIRREL

Cut a slice off the top of the cake to the depth of the hole required. Cut out a hole, slightly off centre and remove, fix the slice back to the cake with boiling apricot purée. Cover with almond paste in the normal way.

1 Prepare the cake, then cover with mottled sugarpaste. Immediately mark with a fork and brush with dusting powder to form bark effect.

2 Using the template as a guide, fill-in the parts shown with royal icing onto non-stick paper. Leave to dry for 10 minutes.

3 Fill-in the remaining parts. Leave to dry for 24 hours. Brush with food colouring as shown.

4 When dry fix the figure to the cake-top. Make and fix a sugarpaste nut.

5 Decorate the cake with sugarpaste leaves, nuts and fruits together with piped sugar flowers as required.

INGREDIENTS

25.5cm round cake (10in)
1.25k almond paste (2½lb)
1.75k sugarpaste (3½lb)
450g royal icing (1lb)
Confectioner's varnish
Assorted dusting powders
Assorted food colours

EQUIPMENT and DECORATIONS

33cm round cake board (13in)
Fork
Non-stick paper
Fine paint brush
Sugarpaste leaves, nuts and fruits
Piped sugar flowers
Board edge ribbon

PAINT POT

15cm round sponge (6in) 4 required
1.5k sugarpaste (3lb)
115g royal icing (4oz)
Assorted food colours

30.5cm round cake board (12in)
15cm round cake board (6in)
Piping tubes No.1 and 2

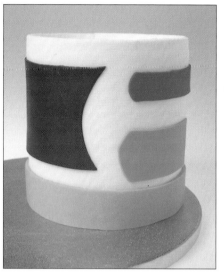

1 Layer and fill the sponges together, coat the outside with buttercream and refrigerate for 1 hour. Place the cake board on top then cover the whole side with sugarpaste. Leave to dry for 2 hours.

2 Remove the top cake board. Cut out and fix various sugarpaste shapes to the cake-side.

3 Cut and fix a sugarpaste ring on the cake-top. Roll out two colours of sugarpaste to form striped paint effect and fix to the cake-side, as shown.

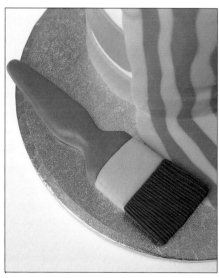

4 Cut and fix the same two colours of sugarpaste in a swirl onto the cake-top.

5 Make and place a sugarpaste paint brush onto the board.

6 Pipe "STRIPED PAINT" onto the cake-side with royal icing (No.2). Make and fix a sugarpaste 'splash' with piped inscription of choice (No.1).

THE GOLFER

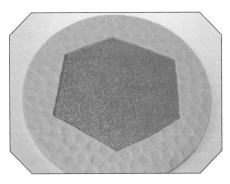

1 Cover the cake board with sugarpaste then, using the end of a small rolling pin, indent the paste as shown. Cut out the area to be covered by the cake.

2 Cover the cake with mottled sugarpaste and fix onto the board. When dry, paint the scenery shown.

INGREDIENTS

23cm hexagonal cake (9in)
1.75k sugarpaste (3½lb)
115g royal icing (4oz)
Assorted food colours

EQUIPMENT and DECORATIONS

33cm round cake board (13in)
Piping tube No.1
Fine paint brush
Small rolling pin
Board edge ribbon

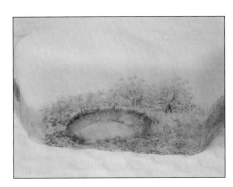

3 Paint the bunker scenery on the next panel.

4 Paint the fairway and green. Then repeat the paintings on the remaining sides.

114

5 Using the template as a guide, mould sugarpaste pieces as shown onto greaseproof paper.

6 Mould and fix the remaining pieces then transfer to the cake-top. Paint in the ground.

7 Pipe message of choice with royal icing (No.1).

BATH TUB

INGREDIENTS

Sponge baked in a 450g loaf tin (1lb)
900g sugarpaste (2lb)
115g royal icing (4oz)
Pink dusting powder
Assorted food colours

EQUIPMENT and DECORATIONS

30.5 x 20.5cm oblong cake board (12 x 8in)
Piping tubes No.1 and 2
Grater
Paint brush
Board edge ribbon

1 Cover the top of the cake with sugarpaste.

2 Upturn the cake onto an icing sugar dusted surface. Layer, then cover with sugarpaste. Trim around the sides to leave a rim. Leave to dry for 2 hours.

3 Roll out and cut mottled sugarpaste and white sugarpaste squares to cover the board. Cut out a bath base and then mould and shape four feet. Leave until dry.

4 Mould and shape sugarpaste neck and shoulders, head, toes and taps. Leave until dry. Decorate the head with food colours and dusting powder.

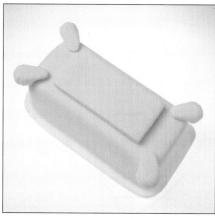

5 Fix the base and feet to the bath tub.

6 Fix the squares to the cake board. Carefully upturn the bath tub and fix in position shown. Stipple the top with royal icing.

7 Fix the head and shoulders then brush royal icing around the edge.

8 Fix the taps and feet. Make and fix any other items of fun.

9 Make a sugarpaste bath towel and place onto the floor. Pipe inscription of choice (No.2 and 1).

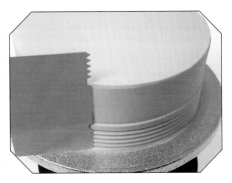

1 Coat the cake with royal icing. Use a scraper cut to the pattern shown for the final coating of the cake-side. Leave to dry for 24 hours.

2 Using the templates as a guide, outline (No.1) and flood-in as many runouts onto non-stick paper as required. Leave to dry for 24 hours.

3 Pipe the curved lines shown (No.2 and 1). Fix the runouts, then complete the inscriptions (No.2 and 1).

4 Pipe 'C' scrolls around part of the cake-top edge (No.43).

5 Pipe shells around the remaining cake-top edge and base (No.43). Overpipe the shells (No.2 and 1). Fix runouts to the cake board.

INGREDIENTS

20.5cm round cake (8in)
680g almond paste (1½lb)
680g royal icing (1½lb)
Pink and green food colours

EQUIPMENT

28cm round cake board (11in)
Piping tubes No.1, 2 and 43
Non-stick paper
Patterned side scraper

FIFTY TO-DAY

1 Cover the cake and board with sugarpaste. Cut butterfly wings from modelling paste. Leave to dry 1 hour, outline with liquid colours, then fill-in with dusting powders.

2 Lightly trace the branch onto the cake-top. Brush embroider the parts shown (see glossary).

3 Complete the brush embroidery as shown.

INGREDIENTS

20.5cm round cake (8in)
680g almond paste (1½lb)
680g sugarpaste (1½lb)
115g modelling paste (4oz)
115g royal icing (4oz)
Assorted dusting powders
Assorted food colours

For the brush embroidery piping:

Mix 1tsp of piping gel with 4tbsp
 of royal icing.
Colour as required.

EQUIPMENT and DECORATIONS

25.5cm round cake board (10in)
Piping tubes No.1 and 2
Paint brush
Stamens
Board edge ribbon

4 Trace the wings onto the cake-side.
Then colour with dusting powders.

5 Mould a butterfly body from
modelling paste, fix to the cake-top
with the wings. Support if
necessary until set. Insert two
stamens for antennae.

6 Pipe shells around the cake-base
with royal icing (No.2) then pipe a
line over the shells (No.1). Pipe
inscription of choice (No.1).

Retirement

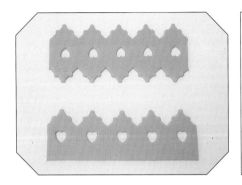

1 Cover the cake and board with sugarpaste. Using the template as a guide, cut out sugarpaste design, or use appropriate shaped cutters.

2 Fix the sugarpaste to the top-edge and base of the cake.

3 Using the template as a guide, cut out the various parts for the shed from modelling paste. Stipple the roof with royal icing and sprinkle with granulated sugar. Leave until dry.

20.5cm oblong octagonal shaped
  cake (8in)
900g sugarpaste (2lb)
225g royal icing (8oz)
225g modelling paste (8oz)
Granulated sugar
Assorted food colours

25.5cm oblong octagonal board (10in)
Piping tubes No.1 and 2
Continuous cutter
Plastic figures
Board edge ribbon

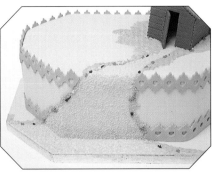

4 When dry, assemble and fix the shed then pipe the shells as shown, with royal icing (No.2).

5 Fix the shed to the cake top, stipple the grass and then filigree the path as shown (No.1).

6 Remove some edging and continue path down cake-side onto board. Pipe dots (No.1). Make and fix items. Pipe inscription (No.1).

25.5cm square cake (10in)
1.5k almond paste (3lb)
1.5k royal icing (3lb)
Pink and lilac food colours

35.5cm square cake board (14in)
Piping tubes No.1, 2 and 7
Narrow ribbons

Floral spray
Sugar birds
Board edge ribbon

1 Coat the cake and board with royal icing. When dry, pipe scrolls along two sides of the cake-top edge (No.7).

2 Pipe shells around the remaining cake-top edges and base (No.7).

3 Pipe a line beside the scrolls and a rope line beside the shells on the cake-top (No.2).

4 Pipe rope lines on the cake-side and board as shown (No.2).

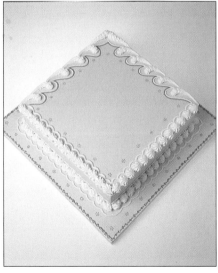

5 Pipe a line beside the scroll line, dots on the cake-top and board, then a filigree line on the board edge (No.1).

6 Fix the floral spray onto the cake-top. Pipe and decorate the inscription with tracery (No.1). Decorate the cake with birds and ribbon bows.

CANDLE-LIGHT

INGREDIENTS

Large swiss roll
680g sugarpaste (1lb)
225g royal icing (8oz)
60g modelling paste (2oz)
Assorted dusting powders
Assorted food colours

EQUIPMENT and DECORATIONS

Suitably sized saucer
Soft brush
Christmas spray and ribbon

1 Cover the swiss roll with sugarpaste, shaping the end to form candle.

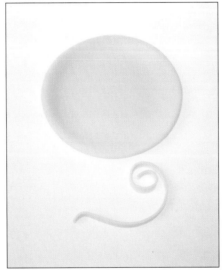

2 Cover the saucer with sugarpaste, then make a handle from modelling paste. Leave to dry for 2 hours.

3 Brush the saucer and handle with various colours of dusting powder.

4 Roll out three colours of sugarpaste to form pear shapes, twist together to form the candle flame.

5 Fix the candle onto the saucer then fix the handle under the saucer.

6 Pipe softened royal icing onto the candle to form melted wax. Fix the sugarpaste flame. Decorate the candle base with the Christmas spray and ribbon.

CHRISTMAS NIGHT

1 Coat the cake with royal icing and leave until dry. Trace the template onto card and cut out. Place onto the cake-top and spread with royal icing.

2 Immediately remove the card in one continuous movement. Repeat for the cake-side designs.

3 Pipe shells around the cake-top edge and base (No.43). Stipple royal icing around the cake board edge. Pipe inscription (No.2).

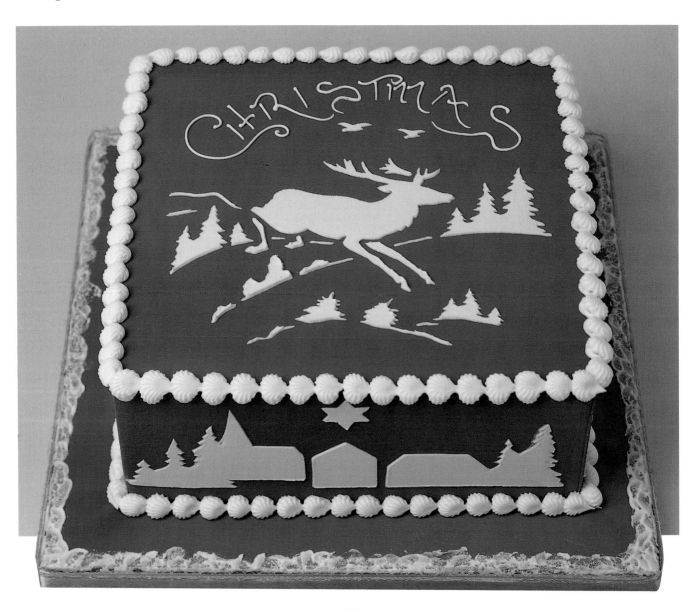

20.5cm square cake (8in)
900g almond paste (2lb)
900g royal icing (2lb)
Blue food colour

EQUIPMENT and DECORATIONS

28cm square cake board (11in)
Piping tubes No.2 and 43
Card for stencil
Board edge ribbon

FAMILY TIME

INGREDIENTS

Swiss roll
680g sugarpaste (1½lb)
225g royal icing (8oz)
Assorted food colours

EQUIPMENT and DECORATIONS

28cm round cake board (11in)
Bone modelling tool
Fine sponge
Piping tube No.1
Board edge ribbon

1 Coat the board with royal icing then stipple with a fine sponge to form the grass. Leave until dry.

2 Cover the swiss roll with sugarpaste to form the tree trunk. Mould paste to root shape and fix to the tree base using a bone tool.

3 Make and fix a sugarpaste branch and door. Pipe ivy, with royal icing, around the door using a piping bag cut to a leaf shape.

4 Using sugarpaste, make a rabbit dressed in the manner shown. Fix to the board when dry.

5 Make another rabbit as shown. Fix to the board when dry.

6 Make and fix a small rabbit to the branch, then a rabbit head with window as shown.

7 Make and fix sugarpaste lanterns then pipe the lines with royal icing (No.1).

8 Stipple royal icing as required to form snow.

9 Make and decorate sugarpaste presents and a broom as shown. Fix ribbon around the board.

INGREDIENTS

20.5cm bell shaped cake (8in)
1.5k sugarpaste (3lb)
225g royal icing (8oz)
Assorted food colours

EQUIPMENT and DECORATIONS

28cm round cake board (11in)
Wire sieve
Piping tubes No.1 and 2
Board edge ribbon

1 Cover the cake and board with sugarpaste. Pipe shells around the cake-base with royal icing (No.2).

2 Push sugarpaste through a wire sieve to form foliage and fix to the cake-side. Decorate with sugarpaste seasonal flowers and nuts. Pipe the berries (No.1).

3 Cut out and fix sugarpaste ribbons and top. Decorate with flowers. Pipe inscription of choice, holly and musical notes onto the cake board (No.1).

FROSTIE

25.5cm oval cake (10in)
900g almond paste (2lb)
680g royal icing (1¼lb)
225g sugarpaste (8oz)
Assorted food colours

33cm oval cake board (13in)
25.5cm oval cake card (10in)
Oblong card
Piping tubes No.1 and 3
Decorative board covering

Christmas motto
Miniature plastic holly
Ribbon bows

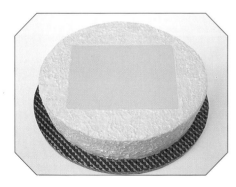

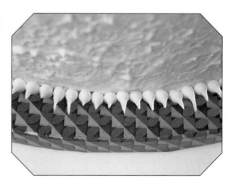

1 Glue covering to board. Coat cake with royal icing. Fix to board with cake card. When dry, place an oblong card on cake-top then stipple cake with royal icing.

2 When dry, remove the card. Cut out and fix sugarpaste shapes as shown. Decorate with royal icing (No.1).

3 Pipe pointed bulbs around the cake-base (No.3). Decorate the cake with holly, motto and bows.

CHRISTMAS SOCKS

INGREDIENTS

2 swiss rolls
1.5k sugarpaste (3lb)
225g royal icing (8oz)
Assorted food colours

EQUIPMENT and DECORATIONS

40.5 x 30.5cm oblong cake
  board (16 x 12in)
Cut cake card to fit socks
Piping tubes No.1 and 2

Decorative board covering
Heart-shaped cutter
Holly leaf cutter
Tartan ribbon

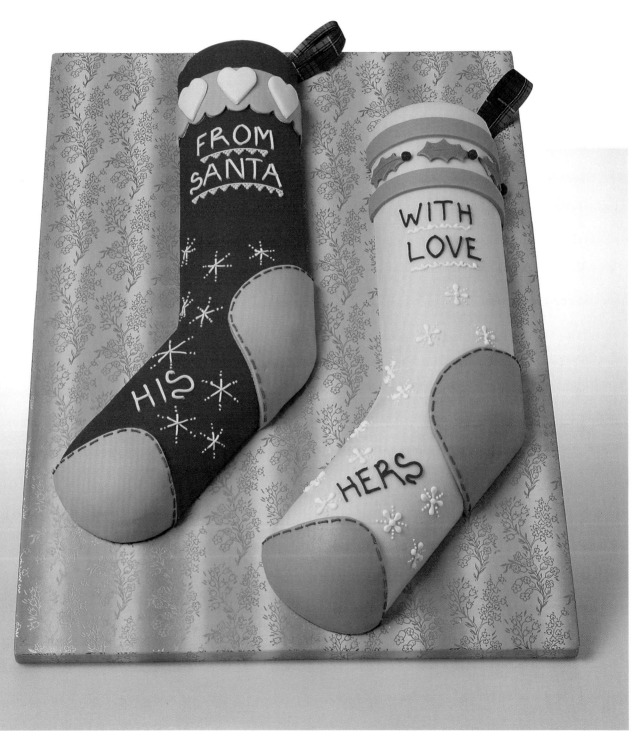

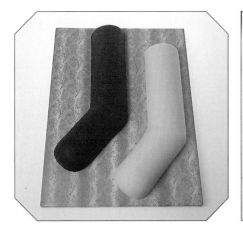
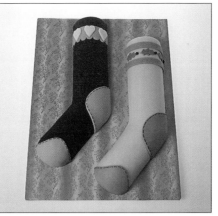

1 Glue covering to board. Slice swiss rolls down the middle, trim to make into two socks. Fix to cake card, then to board. Cover with sugarpaste as shown.

2 Cut out and fix sugarpaste shapes to decorate the socks. Pipe the stitches with royal icing (No.1).

3 Pipe snow flakes (No.1) and messages of choice (No.2). Fix a ribbon loop to each sock top.

SNOW SCENE

INGREDIENTS

20.5cm round cake (8in)
680g almond paste (1½lb)
680g royal icing (1½lb)
Blue and red food colours

EQUIPMENT and DECORATIONS

28cm round cake board (11in)
Piping tubes No.1, 2, 4 and 43
Serrated scraper
Seasonal cake decorations
Board edge ribbon

1 Coat the cake with royal icing. When dry, pipe scrolls (No.43), bulbs (No.4) and icicles (No.2) around the cake-top edge, with royal icing as shown.

2 Overpipe the scrolls (No.2) then pipe a line beside the scrolls (No.2).

3 Pipe shells around the cake-base (No.43). Stipple royal icing around the edge of the cake board. Make a snow scene then pipe message of choice (No.1) on the cake-top.

SKI TRIP

INGREDIENTS

25.5cm round cake (10in)
1.25k almond paste (2½lb)
1.5k sugarpaste (3lb)
450g royal icing (1lb)
Meringue pieces
Assorted food colours

EQUIPMENT and DECORATIONS

33cm round cake board (13in)
Piping tube No.1
Spaghetti strands
Board edge ribbon

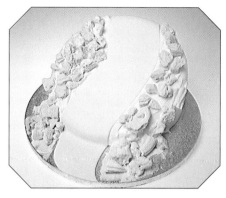

1 Slice the cake at an angle, turn the top slice around, layer and cover with sugarpaste to form slope. Fix broken meringues and coat with royal icing.

2 Make sugarpaste body parts and skiing equipment. Leave until dry.

3 Fix the pieces into the snow using coloured spaghetti for poles. Pipe inscription of choice (No.1).

GREETINGS

1 Coat the cake and board with royal icing. Using the template as a guide, cut out and fix the sugarpaste shape to the cake-top.

2 Pipe shells, with royal icing, around the sugarpaste edge (No.3) then a line over the shells (No.2).

3 Overpipe the No.2 line (No.1) then pipe pointed dots as shown (No.1).

Increase the template to match the size of the cake being used.

20.5cm round cake (8in)   340g sugarpaste (12oz)   25.5cm round cake board (10in)
680g almond paste (1½lb)   Assorted food colours   Piping tubes No.1, 2 and 3
680g royal icing (1½lb)   Seasonal floral spray
                                                     Board edge ribbon

4 Pipe and decorate the inscription (No.1).

5 Repeat steps 2 and 3 around the cake-base.

6 Stipple royal icing over the cake-top and side. Fix the floral spray to the cake-top, then ribbon around the cake board.

NOËL NOËL

1 Cover cake and board with sugar-paste. Leave to dry 24 hours. Mould a cone of almond paste and fix to a cocktail stick. Pipe petals from base up, with royal icing (No.57).

2 Continue piping the petals to form cones. 24 required of varying sizes. Leave until dry.

3 Using sugarpaste, cut out holly leaves, mark the veins and place over a rolling pin to dry. 100 required of varying sizes.

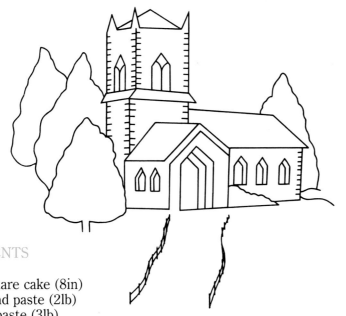

INGREDIENTS

20.5cm square cake (8in)
900g almond paste (2lb)
1.5k sugarpaste (3lb)
225g royal icing (8oz)
60g granulated sugar (2oz)
Assorted dusting powders
Assorted food colours

INGREDIENTS for the cones:

115g almond paste (4oz)
225g royal icing (8oz)

EQUIPMENT and DECORATIONS

28cm square cake board (11in)
Cocktail sticks
Rolling pins
Holly cutters
Fine paint brush
Wide, soft paint brush
Piping tubes No.1 and 57
Board edge ribbon

4 Trace template onto cake top, colour with food colours and dusting powders. When dry, stipple royal icing, using the wide soft brush, over picture for the snow.

5 Fix holly leaves and cones around the picture. Make and fix sugarpaste berries. Stipple with royal icing for the snow.

6 Dust the edge of the cake with dusting powder then pipe snow, with royal icing, around the cake-top edge. Sprinkle granulated sugar over the snow.

7 Repeat step 5 around the cake-base.

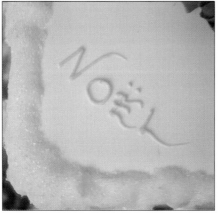

8 Pipe message on two corners of the cake-top (No.1).

9 Pipe bells on the other corners (No.1). Fix the ribbon around the cake board edge.

INGREDIENTS

23 x 15cm oblong shaped
  cake (9 x 6in)
1.25k almond paste (2½lb)
1.25k sugarpaste (2½lb)
225g modelling paste (8oz)
225g royal icing (8oz)
Vegetable fat
Cornflour
Green and black food colours

EQUIPMENT and DECORATIONS

33cm square cake board (13in)
Large bell moulds
Small bell moulds
Narrow ribbons
Floral wire
Filling flowers
Piping tubes No.1, 2 and 3
Miniature crackers
Board edge ribbon

1 Cover the cake and board with sugarpaste. Lightly grease the bell mould with white fat. Sift cornflour into the mould and tap out the surplus, to leave a light dusting over the fat.

2 Mould some modelling paste into a ball, insert into the mould and press the paste to cover the inside of the mould, at an even thickness.

3 After a few minutes, tap the mould to release the bell. 2 large and 8 small bells required. When dry, pipe filigree over the bells, with royal icing (No.1).

4 Make a selection of ribbon loops by folding the ribbon and twisting wire around the base.

5 Fix modelling paste into the bells to half full. Insert the ribbon loops and filling flowers, as shown.

6 Pipe shells around the cake-base, with royal icing, and scrolls around the cake-top edge (No.3).

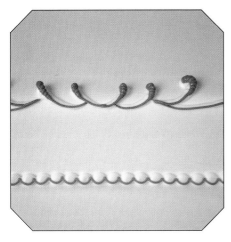

7 Pipe a line over the shells and overpipe the scrolls.

8 Fix the large bells onto the cake-top. Pipe inscription of choice and then decorate with filigree and piped musical notes (No.1).

9 Pipe a filigree line around the cake board edge (No.1). Fix the small bells onto the cake board corners and crackers between. Pipe musical notes (No.1).

CELEBRATION

INGREDIENTS

25.5cm square cake (10in)
1.5k almond paste (3lb)
2k sugarpaste (4lb)
225g royal icing (8oz)
Cream and brown food colours

EQUIPMENT and DECORATIONS

35.5cm square cake board (14in)
Piping tube No.1
Endless lace cutter
Embosser
Crimper

Floral sprays
Narrow ribbon
Miniature gold horseshoes
Medium gold horseshoes
Board edge ribbon

1 Cut a wedge from the corner of the cake then cover the cake and board with sugarpaste. Crimp around the cake board edge. When dry, fix ribbon around the cake-base.

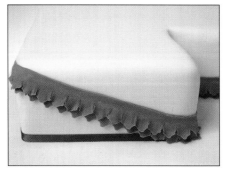

2 Cut out, frill and fix two strips of fluted sugarpaste band to the cake-sides.

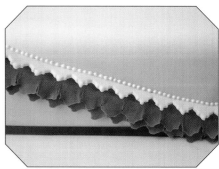

3 Cut out and fix sugarpaste edging. Pipe shells as shown with royal icing (No.1). Decorate the cake as required.

CONGRATULATIONS

INGREDIENTS

23cm heart shaped cake (9in)
1.25k sugarpaste (2½lb)
Cream and brown food colours

EQUIPMENT and DECORATIONS

28cm round cake board (11in)
Piping tube No.1
Leaf cutter
Crimper

Narrow ribbons
Medium gold keys
Board edge ribbon

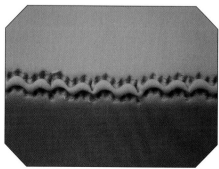

1 Cover the cake and board with two colours of sugarpaste. Immediately crimp around the cake-top edge and board.

2 Fix narrow ribbons across the cake. Cut out and fix sugarpaste leaves around the cake-base.

3 Cut out and fix further leaves then decorate with ribbon loops to form a spray. Pipe inscription of choice (No.1). Fix keys, then ribbon around the board.

ENGAGEMENT

INGREDIENTS

20.5cm heart shaped cake (8in)
680g almond paste (1½lb)
900g sugarpaste (2lb)
115g modelling paste (4oz)
450g royal icing (1lb)
Confectioner's varnish
Assorted dusting powders
Assorted food colours

EQUIPMENT and DECORATIONS

28cm heart shaped cake
  board (11in)
Piping tubes No.1 and 2
Non-stick paper
Narrow dowling
Miniature flower cutters
Fine paint brushes
Board edge ribbon

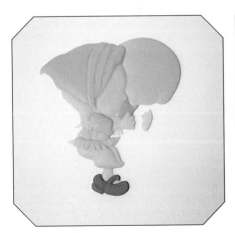

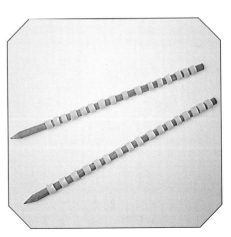

1 Cover the cake and board with sugarpaste. Leave to dry for 24 hours. Pipe-in the figures with royal icing onto non-stick paper. Leave to dry for 24 hours.

2 When dry, brush dusting powder onto the cheeks then paint as shown.

3 Cut out strips of modelling paste, cut into small lengths and place over narrow dowells. Leave to dry then brush with confectioner's varnish.

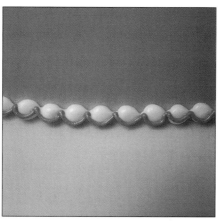

4 Trace the window, table and chair onto the cake-top and brush-in with dusting powders and food colours.

5 Pipe shells around the cake-base with royal icing (No.2). Pipe a line over the shells (No.1).

6 Pipe curved lines around the cake-side (No.2). Pipe a scalloped line under the No.2 line (No.1). Pipe bows (No.1). Pipe a scalloped line around the cake board edge (No.1).

7 Make small cuts around the cake-top edge and insert the curved pieces. Make and fix flowers at the top and bottom.

8 Fix the figures to the cake-top in the position shown.

147

ANNIVERSARY

INGREDIENTS

20.5cm hexagonal cake (8in)
900g almond paste (2lb)
1.5k sugarpaste (3lb)
225g modelling paste (8oz)
225g royal icing (8oz)
Assorted food colours

EQUIPMENT and DECORATIONS

28cm hexagonal cake board (11in)
Crimper
Flower cutter
Leaf cutter
Floral tape, wire and cotton
Non-stick paper
Piping tubes No.1 and 2
Narrow ribbons
Board edge ribbon

PREPARATION

Cover the sides of the cake with sugarpaste. Then cover the whole cake and board. Cut and remove a circle on each cake-side. Crimp the board edge.

1 Prepare the cake as described. Using the template as a guide, pipe 120 lace pieces with royal icing onto non-stick paper (No.1). Fix ribbon around the cake-base. Paint a picture in each circle.

2 Pipe shells around the inside edge of each circle (No.2).

3 When dry, fix the lace pieces to the edge of the circles.

4 Mould, cut and pull modelling paste to form the blossoms. Then make and insert wired cotton for the stamens and stems. 5 blossoms required.

5 Make and wire buds and blackberries as shown.

6 Make and wire the leaves then tape all together to form the spray. Fix to the cake-top with a modelling paste plaque piped with inscription (No.1).

FIRST ANNIVERSARY

INGREDIENTS

20.5cm round cake (8in)
900g almond paste (2lb)
2k sugarpaste (4lb)
450g modelling paste (1lb)
225g royal icing (8oz)
Lilac food colour

EQUIPMENT and DECORATIONS

38cm oval cake board (15in)
Piping tubes No.1 and 2
Modelling tool
Crimper
Miniature horseshoes
Floral spray
Board edge ribbon

1 Cut the cake in half. Slide one side up and fix together. Place onto the cake board and then cover with sugarpaste. Crimp the edge as shown.

2 Pipe shells, with royal icing, around the cake-base (No.2). Cut and mark, using the modelling tool, a sugarpaste frill. Fix to the cake-side as shown.

3 Cut, mark and fix a second frill. Pipe shells along the top of the frill (No.2).

4 Pipe floral designs onto the cake board (No.1). Fix the floral spray onto the cake-top then pipe and decorate inscription (No.1). Fix the miniature horseshoes.

FRUIT AND FLOWERS

INGREDIENTS

20.5cm square cake (8in)
900g almond paste (2lb)
900g royal icing (2lb)
450g almond paste (1lb)
  for the fruits and mice
85g modelling paste (3oz)
Whole cloves
Granulated sugar
Assorted food colours

EQUIPMENT and DECORATIONS

30.5cm square cake board (12in)
Fine sponge
Cocktail stick
Paint brushes
Floral wire and tape
Plastic strawberry tops
Stamens
Piping tubes No.1, 42 and 44
Board edge ribbon

1 Coat the cake and board with royal icing. Leave until dry then stipple the sides with royal icing, using a fine sponge, as shown.

2 Make and colour a selection of fruits, using almond paste.

3 Pipe shells with royal icing around the cake-base (No.44). Fix the fruits onto the board.

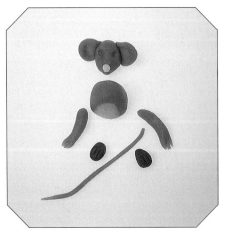

4 Mould the various pieces for the mice, using almond paste. 2 required.

5 Fix the pieces together then decorate with hats and flowers, as shown. Insert stamens for whiskers.

6 Mould the centre of the poppy onto wire, using modelling paste, then insert stamens as shown.

7 Cut modelling paste and frill to make a petal, then fix to wire. Tape four wired petals to the wired centre to form the poppy. 2 poppies required.

8 Mould sugarpaste corn and stems are shown. 3 required. Fix the corn, poppies and mice to the cake-top.

9 Pipe hairs onto the corn (No.1). Pipe shells around the cake-top edge (No.42). Pipe the inscription (No.1).

SILVER YEARS

INGREDIENTS

25.5cm heart shaped cake (10in)
1.5k almond paste (3lb)
1.75k sugarpaste (3½lb)
115g royal icing (4oz)
Edible silver colour
Violet and pink colour mixed together

EQUIPMENT and DECORATIONS

33cm heart shaped cake board (13in)
Plastic beading
Piping tube No.1
Crimped cutter
Sugar doves

Miniature plastic hearts
Small ribbon bow
Board edge ribbon

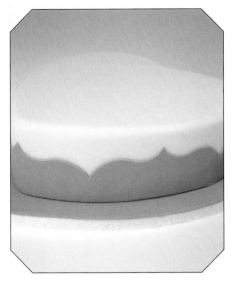

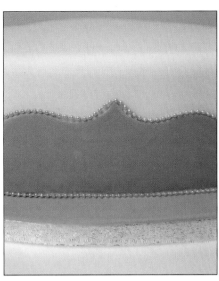

1 Cover the cake with sugarpaste, then cover the board. Using the template as a guide, cut out and fix sugarpaste around the cake-side in the pattern shown.

2 Fix the beading to the cake-side and base.

3 To make a carnation, cut out three discs of sugarpaste using a crimped cutter, then cut small nicks around the edge. Place under polythene to keep moist.

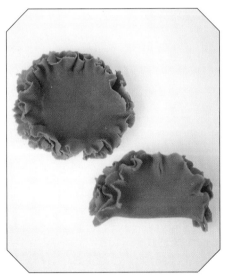

4 Frill the edges, fix the discs together and fold in half.

5 Fold in half again then shape the base to form the flower. 5 blossoms required.

6 Pipe stems and leaves with royal icing, using a leaf shaped piping bag. Then fix carnations, as shown. Pipe and decorate inscription (No.1).

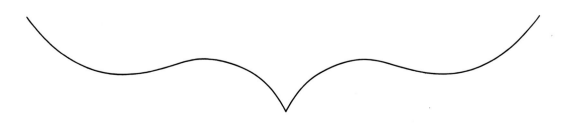

TWENTY-FIVE YEARS

INGREDIENTS

30.5cm petal shaped cake (12in)
2k almond paste (4lb)
2k royal icing (4lb)
Black food colour

NB: use a small amount of black
food colour for light grey
royal icing

EQUIPMENT and DECORATIONS

35.5cm petal shaped cake
  board (14in)
Border nail
Vegetable fat
Piping tubes No.1, 2 and 43
Sugar doves
Plastic 25
Plastic bells
Small artificial flowers and spray
Board edge ribbon

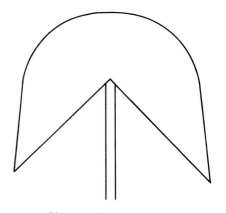

Size and shape of border
nail required.

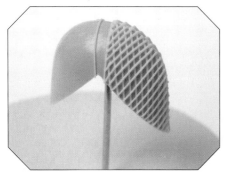

1 Coat the cake and board with royal icing. Pipe the lines shown with royal icing (No.1) onto a lightly greased border nail to form a basket.

2 Repeat piped pattern on other side, pipe shells around edges of each shape. Remove when dry (warm if necessary to release the icing). 7 baskets required.

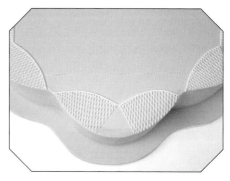

3 Pipe the lattice lines around the cake-top (No.1).

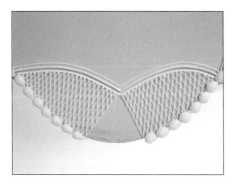

4 Pipe a line beside the lattice (No.2) then a line beside the No.2 line (No.1). Pipe shells around the cake-top edge (No.43) as shown.

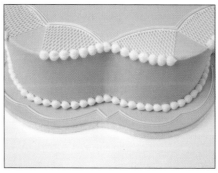

5 Pipe shells around the cake-base (No.43) then pipe lines around the cake board (No.2 and 1).

6 Fix the baskets to the cake-side and decorate with flowers. Decorate the cake with a filled basket, numerals, favours and piped tracery (No.1).

SILVER ANNIVERSARY

1 Coat cake and board with royal icing. Using template as guide, outline (No.1) and flood-in with royal icing onto non-stick paper 4 pieces. Leave to dry 24 hours.

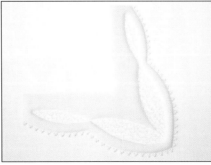

2 When dry, pipe the filigree inside the runout and dots around the outside edge (No.1). Leave to dry for 24 hours.

3 Trace the template onto the cake-top then brush embroider (see glossary) the stems and leaves as shown.

20.5cm square cake (8in)
900g almond paste (2lb)
1.5k royal icing (3lb)
Edible silver colour
Moss green food colour

For the brush embroidery piping:

Mix 1tsp of piping gel with
 4tbsp of royal icing
Colour as required

EQUIPMENT and DECORATIONS

30.5cm square cake board (12in)
Fine paint brush
Non-stick paper
Piping tubes No.1, 2 and 3
Silver lustre
Miniature horseshoes
Board edge ribbon

4 Brush embroider the flower heads.

5 Tilting the cake, repeat steps 3 and 4 for the cake-side design.

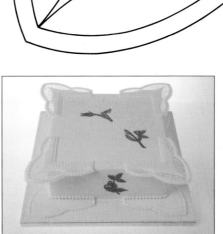

6 Fix the corner runouts to the cake-top. Outline and flood-in matching corners onto the board and leave to dry. Pipe shells around the corners (No.2). Pipe filigree and dots (No.1).

7 Pipe graduated bulbs between the corners (No.3) then a line over the bulbs (No.1). Pipe inscription of choice (No.1) then brush with silver lustre. Fix the horseshoes.

PEARL ANNIVERSARY

1 Coat the cake and board with royal icing. When dry, fix a floral spray to the cake-top and side, as shown. Then, using the templates as a guide, pipe the curved lines shown with royal icing (No.4).

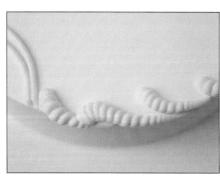

2 Pipe scrolls each side of the curved lines (No.43).

3 Pipe the further scrolls and rosettes as shown (No.43).

4 Pipe a curved rope line around the cake-base (No.43).

5 Pipe graduated dots in each curve around the cake-base, then overpipe the scrolls and rope line (No.2).

25.5cm round cake (10in)
1.25k almond paste (2½lb)
1.25k royal icing (2½lb)
Peach food colour

33cm round cake board (13in)
Piping tubes No.1, 2, 4 and 43
Floral spray
Board edge ribbon

6 Tilt the cake and pipe the curved lines around the cake-side (No.2 and 1).

7 Pipe inscription of choice (No.1) then pipe the tracery (No.1).

8 Pipe the design shown around the edge of the cake board (No.2 and 1).

CORAL ANNIVERSARY

INGREDIENTS

20.5cm round cake (8in)
680g almond paste (1½lb)
900g sugarpaste (2lb)
Salmon pink food colour

EQUIPMENT and DECORATIONS

28cm round cake board (11in)
Crimper
Non-stick paper
Piping tube No.1

Flowers
Sugar birds
Board edge ribbon

1 Cover the cake and board with sugarpaste. Crimp around the board edge. Pipe shells, with royal icing, around the cake-base (No.1). Leave to dry for 24 hours.

2 Pipe lace pieces onto non-stick paper, with royal icing (No.1). 60 pieces required. Leave to dry for 24 hours.

3 Cut and flute a strip of sugarpaste then fix around the cake, as shown.

4 Cut, flute and fix a second, narrower strip of sugarpaste as shown.

5 Carefully fix the lace to the top edge of the frill, using royal icing.

6 Pipe inscription of choice onto the cake-top (No.1). Decorate the cake with flowers and sugar birds.

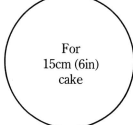

For
15cm (6in)
cake

For
20.5cm (8in)
cake

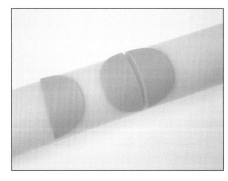

1 Cut circles of modelling paste in half and place over rolling pins to dry. 30 of each size required. Using the template as a guide, pipe lace onto non-stick paper with royal icing (No.1). 200 required.

2 Using modelling paste, make a selection of wired flowers and buds. When dry brush with gold colouring mixture.

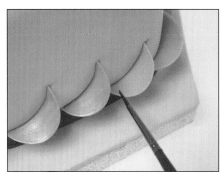

3 When the circles are dry, cover the cakes and board with sugarpaste. Fix ribbon around the cake-base then push the circles into the cake-side. Brush with gold colouring mixture.

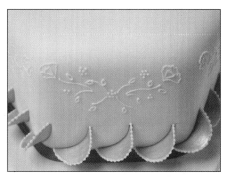

4 Pipe the floral design on each cake-side and then pipe shells on edge of each circle, as shown (No.1).

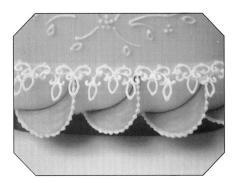

5 Fix the piped lace around the cake-side.

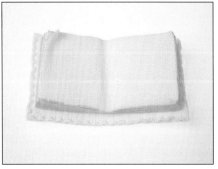

6 Make and decorate a sugarpaste book.

7 Fix the flowers into a sugarpaste plaque to form a spray. Fix to the cake-top with the book.

INGREDIENTS

20.5cm hexagonal cake (8in)
15cm hexagonal cake (6in)
1.75k almond paste (3½lb)
2k sugarpaste (4lb)
450g modelling paste (1lb)
225g royal icing (8oz)
Assorted food colours

EQUIPMENT and DECORATIONS

28cm hexagonal cake board (11in)
20.5cm hexagonal cake board (8in)
Small rolling pin
Flower cutter
Round cutters
Non-stick paper
Piping tube No.1
Fine paint brush
Floral wire and tape
Stamens
Gold lustre mixed with clear
  alcohol for the circles and flowers
Narrow ribbons
Gypsophilia (dried)
Board edge ribbon

25.5cm round cake (10in)
15cm round cake (6in)
2k almond paste (4lb)
2k royal icing (4lb)
1 egg white
Caster sugar

35.5cm round cake board (14in)
23cm round cake board (9in)
Piping tubes No.2, 42 and 43
Crystallised chrysanthemums

Gypsophila (dried)
Narrow ribbons
Gold bells, numerals and motto
Board edge ribbon

1 Coat the cakes and boards with royal icing. When dry, fix narrow ribbons around the cake-sides.

2 Fix crystallised flowers and pieces of coloured dried gypsophila to the cakes as required.

3 Pipe 'S' and 'C' scrolls around the cake-top edge (No.43) with royal icing.

4 Pipe shells around the cake-base (No.42). Pipe a line over the shells (No.2).

5 Pipe 'C' scrolls around the cake board edge (No.42).

6 Fix the motto to the top tier and bells with ribbon loops, as shown.

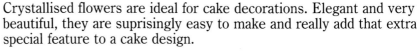

1 Mix 2 teaspoons cold water with 1 fresh egg white. Gently brush the flower petals with solution using soft, medium paint brush.

Crystallised flowers are ideal for cake decorations. Elegant and very beautiful, they are suprisingly easy to make and really add that extra special feature to a cake design.

Before starting check that the flowers you intend to crystallise are edible and have not been sprayed with pesticide.

There are many edible flowers and leaves to choose from and you will probably find a selection in the garden (see list below). Flowers from any bulb such as daffodils, snowdrops or lily-of-the-valley should never be used.

Carefully select the flowers you intend to crystallise and pick when they have just opened and are completely dry (usually around midday). Make sure that they are free from insects and discard any that are not perfect.

The flowers crystallised by the method shown here should be used within a few days. However, if you want flowers to last much longer, they may be prepared by dissolving one teaspoon of gum arabic in 25ml (1fl. oz) of water or clear alcohol such as vodka. Then paint each petal with the mixture and proceed as from step 2 shown on this page. Flowers crystallised in this manner will keep for several months.

Crystallised flowers make very attractive winter decorations when fresh flowers are hard to find for cakes and may also be used for place or table settings.

Crystallised flowers are very fragile and should be handled with extreme care. For that reason, it is wise to crystallise extra flowers in case of breakage.

2 Sprinkle with caster sugar and shake off excess. Coat the back of the petals with the egg white and water solution.

CRYSTALLISING THROUGH THE SEASONS

SPRING	AUTUMN	Nasturtium
Almond blossom	Clove pink	Passionflower
Apple blossom	Nasturtium	Pink
Chamomile	Pansy	Rose
Cherry blossom	Single	Rosemary
Daisy	Chrysanthemum	Scented Leaf
Heartsease		Pelagonium
Honeysuckle	SUMMER	
Japonica	Borage	WINTER
Lemon Balm	Carnation	Jasmine
Majoram	Chive	Freesia
Mint	Cornflower	
Pansy	Evening Primrose	
Parsley	Hibiscus	
Pear blossom	Honeysuckle	
Polyanthus	Hyssop	
Primula	Jasmin	
Primrose	Lavender	
Sage	Lime Marigold	
Violet	Mimosa	

3 Sprinkle with caster sugar. Place flowers on wire tray for 24 hours to dry.

GOLDEN YEARS

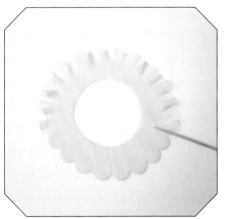

1 Cover cake and board with sugarpaste. When dry, pipe shells, using royal icing, around cake-base (No.2). Cut out sugarpaste circle and flute edge with a cocktail stick.

2 Cut and fix the frill to the cake-side curve as shown.

3 Make and fix frills to the remaining sides. Leave until dry. Fix material lace against the top edge of the frills.

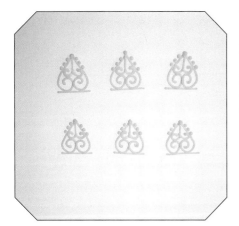

INGREDIENTS

25.5cm petal shaped cake (10in)
1.5k almond paste (3lb)
2k sugarpaste (4lb)
450g royal icing (1lb)
Cream and peach food colours

EQUIPMENT and DECORATIONS

33cm round cake board (13in)
Non-stick paper
Cocktail stick
Piping tubes No.1 and 2
Material lace
Spray of sugarpaste flowers
Narrow ribbon
Plastic numeral
Board edge ribbon

4 Pipe lace pieces onto non-stick paper with royal icing (No.1). 60 pieces required. Leave until dry.

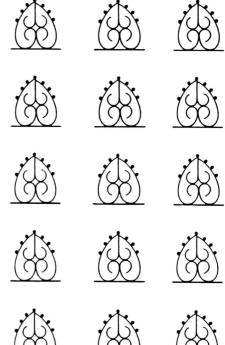

5 When dry, fix the piped lace to the top edge of the material lace using royal icing.

6 Pipe the floral design shown on each cake-side curve and then around the board (No.1).

7 Pipe the curved lines shown on each cake-top curve (No.1).

8 Fix a floral spray of sugarpaste flowers to the cake-top.

9 Pipe and decorate inscription of choice (No.1).

DIAMOND ANNIVERSARY

INGREDIENTS

28cm heart shaped cake (11in)
2k almond paste (4lb)
2k sugarpaste (4lb)

225g royal icing (8oz)
Assorted food colours

EQUIPMENT and DECORATIONS

35.5cm heart shaped cake board (14in)
Piping tubes No.1, 2 and 43
Assorted flowers
Board edge ribbon

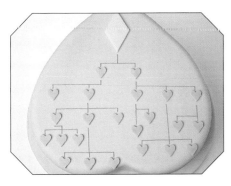

1 Cover the cake and board with sugarpaste then leave until dry. Pipe family tree onto the cake-top with royal icing (No.1). Cut out and fix sugarpaste hearts and diamond.

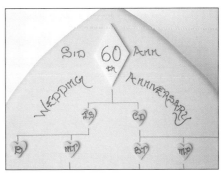

2 Pipe all the initials, names and anniversary (No.1).

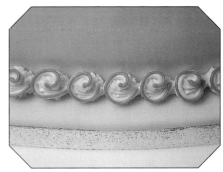

3 Pipe shells around the cake-base (No.43). Pipe a 'C' line onto each shell (No.2) then overpipe the lines (No.1). Decorate the cake with flowers of choice.

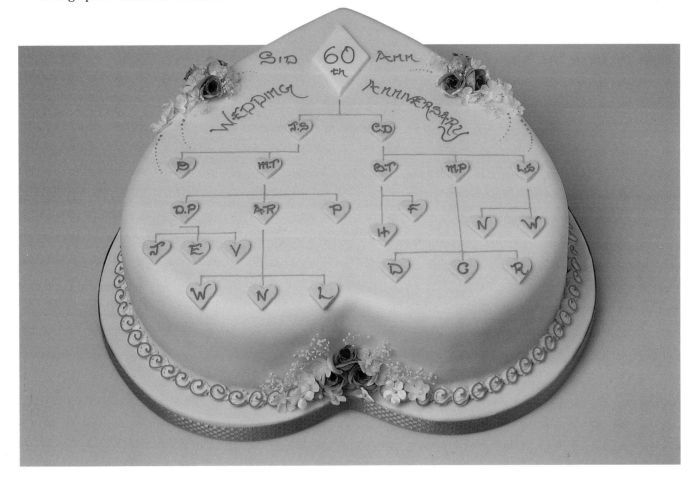

WHITE ORCHID

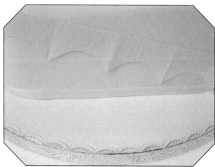

1 Make bridge sections. Cover cake with sugarpaste. Crimp around board edge. Fix ribbon. Cut a paper template into 4 curved sections and mark the cake-side as shown.

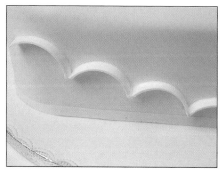

2 Fix the bridge sections into the cake-sides.

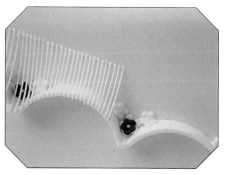

3 Make and fix small sugarpaste flowers. Pipe lines from the cake-side to the bridge edge, as shown (No.1). Pipe shells on the edges of the bridge (No.1).

INGREDIENTS

20.5cm fan shaped cake (8in)
900g almond paste (2lb)
900g sugarpaste (2lb)
450g modelling paste (1lb)
Black food colour

EQUIPMENT and DECORATIONS

28cm round cake board (11in)
Rolling pins
Crimper
Non-stick paper
Blossom cutters
Flower cutters
Floral wire and tape
Narrow ribbon
Piping tubes No.0, 1 and 2
Board edge ribbon

PREPARATION of BRIDGE SECTIONS

Cut 8 strips of modelling paste 12mm (½in) wide. Place over a curved mould to match the length and curve of the template. Leave to dry for 24 hours before covering the cake with sugarpaste.

4 Using the template as a guide, pipe the lace, with royal icing onto non-stick paper (No.1). 60 pieces required. Leave until dry.

5 Pipe the lines and dots shown on the cake-top (No.0 or 1).

6 Fix the lace to the cake as shown.

7 Cut and shape the parts shown from modelling paste, to make an orchid.

8 Fix the pieces together, leave to dry, then colour as required.

9 Make sufficient orchids and filler flowers to form a spray for the cake-top.

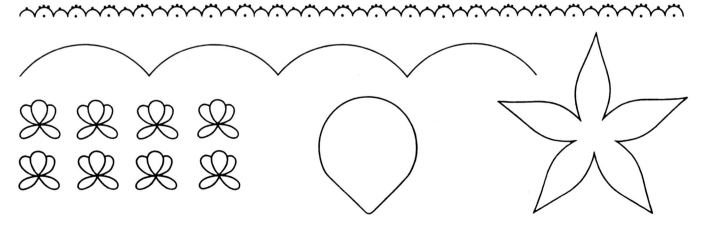

173

1 Cover the cake and board with sugarpaste. Leave to dry for 24 hours. Trace the templates onto the cake-top to make a floral spray as required. Start to brush embroidery (see glossary) the design (No.2).

2 Complete the brush embroidery as shown.

3 Cut out sugarpaste petal shape and flute the top edge with a cocktail stick.

4 Lightly dust the edge then fix around the cake-base. Continue making and fixing the petals to complete the base.

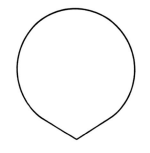

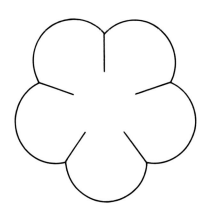

INGREDIENTS

25.5cm round cake (10in)
1.25k almond paste (2½lb)
1.5k sugarpaste (3lb)
450g modelling paste (1lb)
225g royal icing (8oz)
Pink dusting powder
Green food colour

For the brush embroidery piping:

Mix 1tsp of piping gel with 4tbsp of royal icing.
Colour as required

EQUIPMENT and DECORATIONS

33cm round cake board (13in)
Paint brush
Flower cutters
Leaf cutters
Ring moulds
Cocktail stick
Piping tube No.2
Floral wire and tape
Corn silk
Board edge ribbon

WILD ROSE

5 Wire corn silk then tape up to form the flower centre. Cut out and flute modelling paste petals as shown.

6 Place the petals in ring moulds for shaping. Make a hole in the centre then leave until dry.

7 Thread the wire through the petals and fix with a little royal icing. Lightly brush with dusting powder. Make buds and leaves, tape together to form the top spray.

INGREDIENTS

25.5cm heart shaped cake (10in)
20.5cm heart shaped cake (8in)
2.5k almond paste (5lb)
2.5k royal icing (5lb)
Lemon and caramel food colours

EQUIPMENT and DECORATIONS

33cm heart shaped cake board (13in)
25.5cm heart shaped cake board (10in)
Non-stick paper
Piping tubes No.0, 1, 2 and 3
Miniature horseshoes
Leaves and flowers
Board edge ribbon

1 Coat the cake and board with royal icing. Pipe the lace, using the template as a guide, onto non-stick paper with royal icing (No.0 or 1). 180 pieces required. Leave until dry.

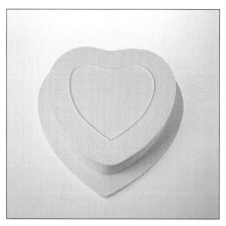

2 Make a heart template and place onto the cake-top. Pipe a line around the template edge (No.2) then overpipe the line (No.2). Pipe filigree around the outside edge (No.1). Remove the template.

3 Pipe bulbs around the cake-base (No.2). Then pipe filigree around the edge of the cake board (No.1).

4 Pipe a line over the bulbs (No.1).

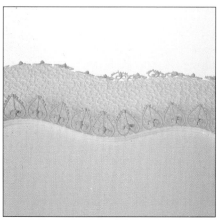

5 Fix the lace to the top of the No.2 line on the cake-top, to lean up and out.

6 Fix the lace to the edge of the cake-top, tilting the cake to fix. Decorate the cake with leaves and flowers as required.

HORSESHOE WEDDING

INGREDIENTS

30.5cm horseshoe shaped cake
  (12in)
20.5cm horseshoe shaped cake
  (8in)
2k almond paste (4lb)
1.5k sugarpaste (3lb)
900g royal icing (2lb)
Pink and green food colour

EQUIPMENT and DECORATIONS

35.5cm horseshoe shaped cake
  board (14in)
25.5cm horseshoe shaped cake
  board (10in)
Non-stick paper
Piping tubes No.1, 2, 42 and 43
Floral sprays
Wishbones
Narrow ribbon
Board edge ribbon

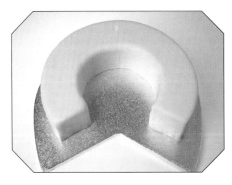

1 Cover the cakes with sugarpaste. Leave to dry for 24 hours.

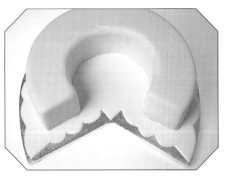

2 Pipe a decorative line around the cake board with royal icing (No.2). Then flood-in with softened royal icing. Leave to dry for 24 hours.

3 Outline (No.1) and flood-in heart plaques onto non-stick paper with royal icing. 2 of each size required. Leave to dry for 24 hours.

4 Pipe shells around the cake-base (No.43). Pipe a monogram of the initials onto the plaques and dots around the edge (No.1). When dry, fix to each cake end.

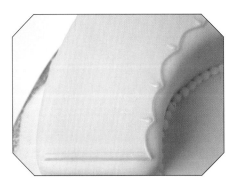

5 Pipe lines along the front and inside top-edge of the cakes (No.2 and 1). Pipe leaf shapes (No.1).

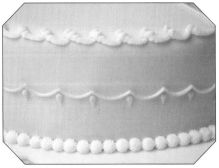

6 Pipe curved lines around the cake-side (No.2 and 1). Pipe leaf shapes (No.1). Pipe scrolls around the cake-top edge (No.42). Decorate the cake with flowers and favours.

179

SPRING WEDDING

INGREDIENTS

25.5cm petal shaped cake (10in)
15cm round cake (6in)
2k almond paste (4lb)
2k sugarpaste (4lb)

225g royal icing (8oz)
570g modelling paste (1¼lb)
Assorted food colours

INGREDIENTS for smocking paste:

450g sugarpaste (1lb)
mixed with
450g modelling paste (1lb)

35.5cm petal shaped cake
  board (14in)
15cm round cake card (6in)
Ribbed roller or expanded straw
Tweezers
Piping tube No.1
Fluted cutter
Miniature heart shaped cutter
Ribbon bows
Floral spray of daffodils, crocuses
  and primoses (see page 182)
Board edge ribbon

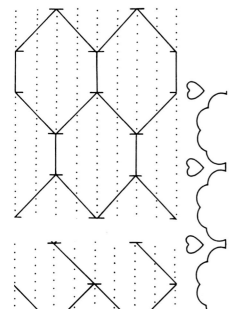

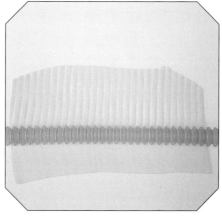

1 Cover the cakes and board with sugarpaste. Leave to dry for 24 hours. Roll out the smocking paste and press with a ribbed roller or expanded plastic straw.

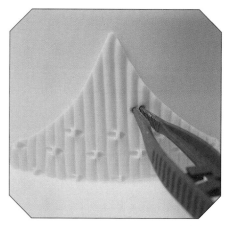

2 Using a paper template cut to size as a guide, cut and fix the paste to cake-side. Squeeze the paste with tweezers to form the marks shown.

3 Pipe diagonal lines then short horizontal lines with royal icing (No.1).

4 Roll out and cut modelling paste into long strips using a fluted round cutter to form the pattern shown. Then cut out small hearts.

5 Fix the strips around the cake-side.

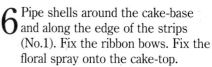

6 Pipe shells around the cake-base and along the edge of the strips (No.1). Fix the ribbon bows. Fix the floral spray onto the cake-top.

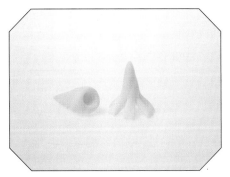

1 **To make a Daffodil:** Mould modelling paste to a cone shape, hollow the centre with a cocktail stick then cut the rim into six sections.

2 Roll out each section with the cocktail stick to form each petal.

3 Mould a thinner, larger cone to form trumpet, tape stamens to wire, insert into the cone and fix, then fix into the petals.

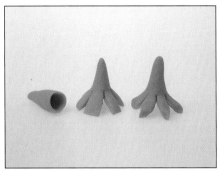

4 **To make a Crocus:** Mould modelling paste into a cone shape, hollow the centre with a cocktail stick. Cut the rim into six sections then squeeze the tips to a point.

5 Roll out each section as shown to form the petals.

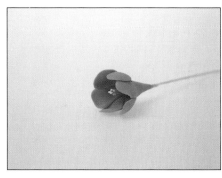

6 Tape stamens to wire, insert into flower and fix.

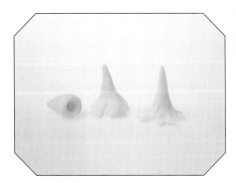

7 **To make a Primrose:** Mould modelling paste to a cone shape, hollow centre using a cocktail stick. Cut the rim into five sections then trim each section into a 'V' shape.

8 Roll out each section with a cocktail stick to form the petals.

9 Push flower onto wire and secure. Mark vein lines with cocktail stick, brush with dusting powder then fix the head of a stamen or pipe royal icing for the centre.

WEDDING DAY

INGREDIENTS

20.5cm round cake (8in)
23cm round cake (9in)
1.75k almond paste (3½lb)
1.75k sugarpaste (3½lb)
 for covering the cake
450g sugarpaste (1lb) mixed with
 5ml gum tragacanth (1tsp) for
 the bridal train and dress
Assorted food colours

EQUIPMENT and DECORATIONS

33cm round cake board (13in)
Endless lace cutter
Crimper
Cocktail stick
Piping tube No.1
Honeysuckle spray
Ribbon loops
Board edge ribbon

1 Cut and cover the cakes with sugarpaste and place onto the cake board as shown, then cover the cake board with sugarpaste and crimp the edge. Leave until dry.

2 Using the template as a guide, cut out the bridegroom from sugarpaste, assemble and leave until dry.

3 Using the template as a guide, cut out the bride from sugarpaste, assemble and leave until dry.

4 Pipe shells around the cake bases with royal icing (No.1). Fix the bride and bridegroom to the cake then cut out and fix a strip of mixed paste for the train support.

5 Cut out and frill, using the mixed paste and fix the train support as shown.

6 Cut and fix the flowing train.

7 Cut and fix the head dress and dress back. Cut out and fix a sugarpaste arch. Pipe the shells as shown (No.1).

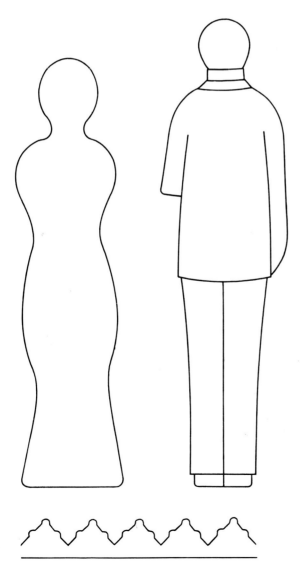

8 Pipe embroidery designs around the cake-side (No.1). Fix a floral spray (see page 185) onto the cake-top with ribbon loops.

HONEYSUCKLE

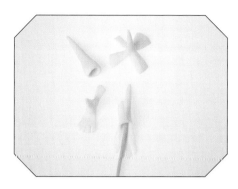

1 Mould modelling paste into a long cone shape. Cut the front into four and spread out. Cut off either side, then cut and flatten front piece. Hollow the inside and shape the top petal.

2 Tape 6 strands of sewing cotton to 26 gauge wire for the stamens. Push through the centre of the flower and fix. Mould and fix paste to wire, to form the buds.

3 Repeat steps 1 and 2 for number of flowers and buds required. Make and wire paste leaves. When all dry, colour with dusting powders as required. Tape together with dried gypsophila to form the spray.

WHITE WEDDING

1 Cover the cakes with sugarpaste. Cut out and fix sugarpaste onto the board and crimp as shown.

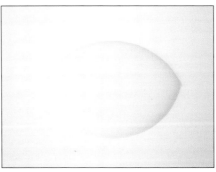

2 Outline (No.1) and flood-in plaques with royal icing onto non-stick paper. 8 required. Leave to dry for 24 hours.

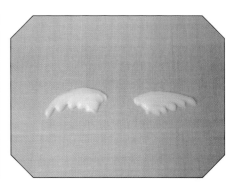

3 Pipe birds' wings onto non-stick paper (No.1). 16 pairs required. Leave to dry for 12 hours.

4 When the wings are dry, pipe the bodies and tails onto non-stick paper (No.1) then immediately insert the wings. Leave to dry.

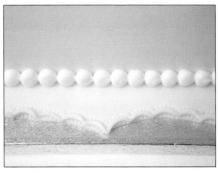

5 Pipe shells around the cake-base (No.3).

6 Pipe scrolls over the shells (No.1).

7 When dry, pipe initials on the plaques and dots around the edge (No.1). When dry, fix to the cake-sides. Fix floral sprays as shown.

8 Pipe tracery onto the cake-top corners (No.2). Fix the sugar birds as required.

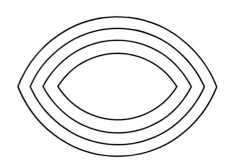

15cm square cake (6in)   23cm square cake board (9in)   Crimper
25.5cm square cake (10in)   33cm square cake board (13in) Piping tubes No.1, 2 and 3
2.5k almond paste (5lb)   Non-stick paper   Floral sprays
2.5k sugarpaste (5lb)
680g royal icing (1½ lb)

INGREDIENTS

18cm round cake (7in)
25.5cm round cake (10in)
2k almond paste (4lb)
2k royal icing (4lb)
Apricot and green food colours

EQUIPMENT and DECORATIONS

23cm round cake board (9in)
35.5cm round cake board (14in)
18cm round cake card (7in)
25.5cm round cake card (10in)
2 round cake boards for initial
  coating
Patterned lace material
Stapler
Glue
Piping tubes No.1, 2, 3 and 43
Narrow ribbon
Leaves and flowers

1 Cover the cake boards with lace material and staple to the back. Glue a thin cake card to the back then glue a cake card on the front. Coat the cakes with royal icing onto spare boards. Transfer when dry.

2 Divide the cake-top edge into 16 portions. Pipe a curved line between each portion (No.3) on the cake-top and side. Pipe the two further lines shown (No.2 and 1).

3 Pipe the curved lines as shown (No.43).

4 Pipe shells around the cake-base (No.43).

5 Pipe dots and leaves as shown (No.1). Fix ribbon around the cake-side and then decorate as required.

JUNE WEDDING

INGREDIENTS

13cm square cake (5in)
20.5cm square cake (8in)
1.5k almond paste (3lb)
1.5k royal icing (3lb)
Pink food colour

EQUIPMENT and DECORATIONS

20.5cm square cake board (8in)
30.5cm square cake board (12in)
Side scraper cut to shape
Piping tubes No.1, 2, 3, 4 and 57
Flowers
Miniature horseshoes
Narrow ribbons
Board edge ribbon

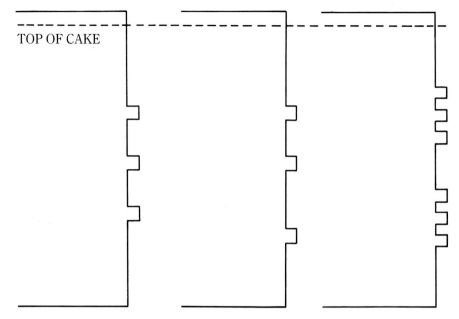

TOP OF CAKE

1 Coat cakes with royal icing, using a scraper cut to pattern shown on the last coat. Leave until dry.

2 Fix ribbons around the cake-sides. Pipe shells around the cake-top and base (No.4).

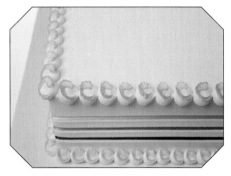

3 Pipe a curved line over each shell (No.57) using two colours of icing in the piping bag.

4 Pipe the lines shown around the cake board (No.3, 2 and 1).

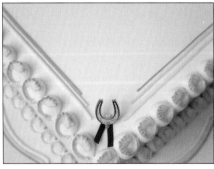

5 Pipe the lines shown around the cake-top (No.3, 2 and 1).

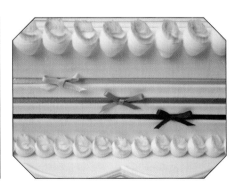

6 Make and fix matching ribbon bows around each cake-side. Fix flowers and horseshoes as required.

HEXAGONAL WEDDING CAKE

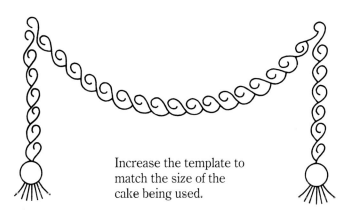

Increase the template to match the size of the cake being used.

INGREDIENTS

15cm hexagonal cake (6in)
20.5cm hexagonal cake (8in)
25.5cm hexagonal cake (10in)
3k almond paste (6lb)
3k royal icing (6lb)
Cream and peach food colours

EQUIPMENT and DECORATIONS

20.5cm hexagonal cake board (8in)
25.5cm hexagonal cake board (10in)
35.5cm hexagonal cake board (14in)
Piping tubes No.1, 2 and 3
Sugarpaste roses and buds
Asparagus fern (dried)
Gypsophila (dried)
Board edge ribbon

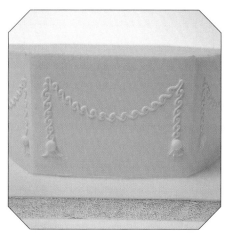

1 Coat the cakes and boards with royal icing. When dry, using the template as a guide, pipe the rope (No.1) and tassels (No.2) onto each cake-side.

2 Pipe scrolls around the cake-top edge (No.3).

3 Pipe the curved lines around the cake-top (No.2) then pipe beside and overpipe the No.2 line (No.1).

4 Pipe a line onto each scroll (No.2).

5 Pipe shells around the cake-base (No.3). Pipe filigree around the cake board edge (No.1).

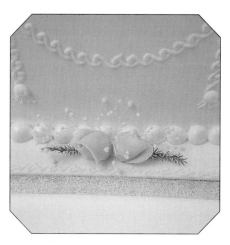

6 Fix sugarpaste rose buds and decorate with dried fern and gypsophilia.

BOUGAINVILLEA WEDDING

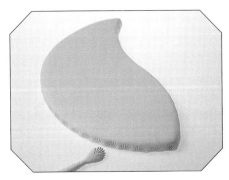
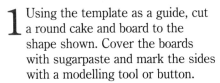

1 Using the template as a guide, cut a round cake and board to the shape shown. Cover the boards with sugarpaste and mark the sides with a modelling tool or button.

2 Cover the cakes with sugarpaste and fix onto the boards. When dry, copy the floral design around each cake side, using edible pens.

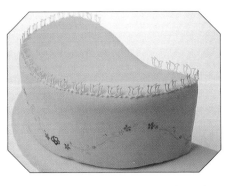

3 Using the template as a guide, pipe the lace onto non-stick paper (No.1). 100 required. When dry fix to the cake-top edge, leaving space for the floral spray.

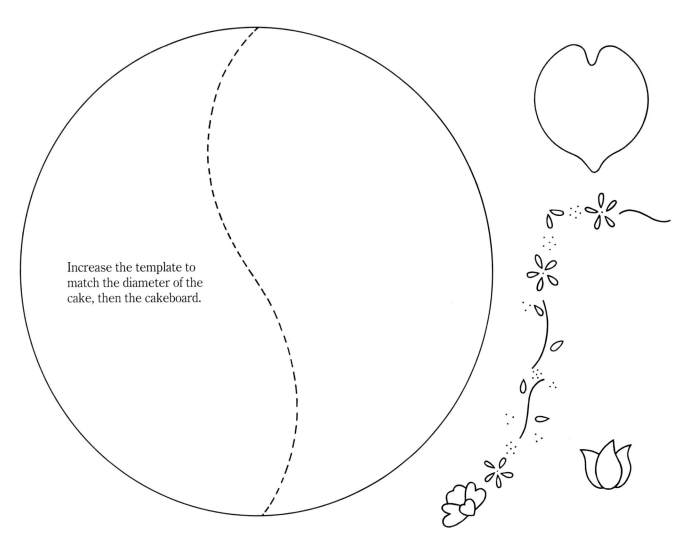

Increase the template to match the diameter of the cake, then the cakeboard.

20.5cm round cake (8in) 2 required
2k almond paste (4lb)
2.5k sugarpaste (5lb)
900g modelling paste (2lb)
Assorted food colours

28cm round cake board (11in)
 2 required
Non-stick paper
Modelling tool
Edible pens

Piping tube No.1
Petal cutter
Floral wire and tape
Various ribbons

4 **To make Bougainvillea:** Mould modelling paste cones onto 3 stamens then fix a tiny blossom onto 1 or 2 heads. Tape together. Cut out and vein 3 bracts, fold and crease the centres.

5 Upturn the bracts, fix bottom edges together and fold back as shown.

6 Tape stamens to wire and thread into the middle of bracts to form the complete flower. Make as many as required then tape into a spray with wired leaves and ribbons.

INGREDIENTS

13cm square cake (5in)
18cm square cake (7in)
25.5cm square cake (10in)
3k almond paste (6lb)
3k royal icing (6lb)
Blue food colour

EQUIPMENT and DECORATIONS

20.5cm square cake board (8in)
25.5cm square cake board (10in)
35.5cm square cake board (14in)
Border nail
Vegetable fat
Piping tubes No.1, 2 and 43
Large horseshoes
Medium horseshoes
Small horseshoes
Floral sprays
Board edge ribbon

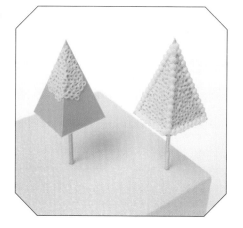

1 Coat cakes and boards with royal icing. Lightly grease a cone border nail, then pipe filigree over two sides with royal icing (No.1). Pipe shells as shown (No.2). 12 corners required.

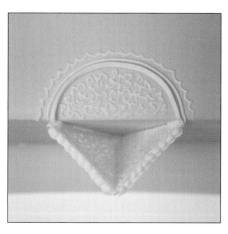

2 When dry, warm cones slightly to remove corners. Fix the corners to the cake-sides. Pipe the curved lines shown (No.2 and 1). Pipe filigree and scalloped line (No.1).

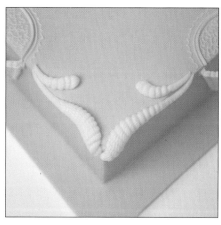

3 Pipe scrolls on the cake-top corners (No.43).

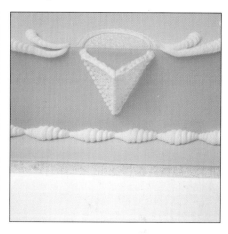

4 Pipe barrel scrolls around the cake-base (No.43).

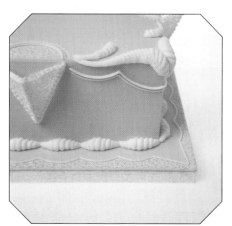

5 Pipe curved lines on the cake sides (No.2 and 1). Pipe curved lines on the cake board (No.2) then filigree as shown (No.1).

6 Decorate the cake with flowers and favours as required.

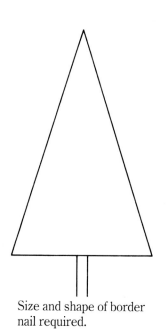

Size and shape of border nail required.

197

INGREDIENTS

15cm oval cake (6in)
20.5cm oval cake (8in)
25.5cm oval cake (10in)
3k almond paste (6lb)
3.5k sugarpaste (7lb)
450g royal icing (1lb)
900g modelling paste (2lb)
Assorted food colours

EQUIPMENT and DECORATIONS

20.5cm oval cake board (8in)
25.5cm oval cake board (10in)
30.5cm oval cake board (12in)
Piping tubes No.1 and 2
Flower cutters

Leaf cutters
Floral wire and tape
Miniature tear-drop cutters
Assorted ribbons
Board edge ribbon

1 Cover the cakes with sugarpaste and then the boards, using a different colour. Fix ribbon around the cake-base. Using the template as a guide, cut out and fix sugarpaste as shown.

2 Using the template as a guide, cut out and fix a second layer of sugarpaste as shown. Leave to dry for 12 hours.

3 Pipe shells, with royal icing, around the cake-top edge (No.2) then pipe rope lines along the edge of each layer of sugarpaste and around the holes.

4 Make a quantity of pulled Jasmin sprays from modelling paste.

5 Using the templates as a guide, make the Christmas Rose calyx and petal as shown. Make the centre of the flower with modelling paste, surround by taped cotton.

6 Make five petals for each rose, fix to the calyx then insert the wired centre.

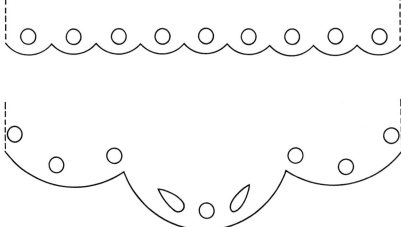

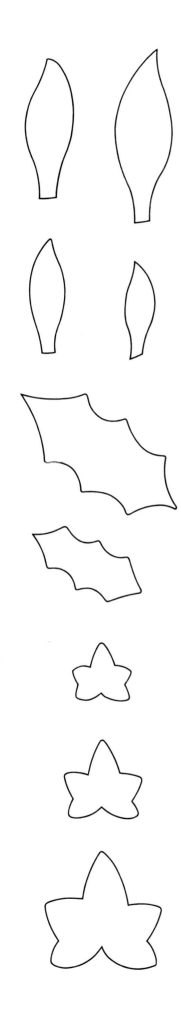

7 Cut out and wire approximately thirty petals of various sizes from modelling paste. Tape cotton to six wires, fix a little modelling paste to each, then tape together.

8 Tape the red, large and medium sized petals to the wired centre.

9 Wire the small and miniature wired petals to the top, then the large green petals behind to complete the flower.

10 Cut out and wire modelling paste holly leaves and berries.

11 Cut out and wire ivy leaves as shown.

12 When dry, tape the flowers and leaves together to complete the sprays, as shown. 1 large, 1 medium and 1 small spray required.

SUMMER WEDDING

INGREDIENTS

15cm round cake (6in)
20.5cm round cake (8in)
25.5cm round cake (10in)
2.5k almond paste (5lb)
2.5k royal icing (5lb)
680g sugarpaste (1½lb)
Assorted food colours

For the brush embroidery piping:

Mix 1tsp of piping gel with
  4tbsp of royal icing.
Colour as required.

EQUIPMENT and DECORATIONS

23cm round cake board (9in)
28cm round cake board (11in)
35.5cm round cake board (14in)
Non-stick paper
Polythene
Fine paint brush
Piping tubes No.0, 1, 2 and 3
Gypsophila (dried)
Narrow ribbons
Board edge ribbon

1 Coat cake and boards with royal icing. Using templates as a guide, pipe the lace with royal icing, onto non-stick paper (No.0 or 1). 180 pieces required. Leave until dry.

2 Divide the cake-side into 4 equal sections. Trace the floral design into each section. Paint in the leaves as shown, using a fine paint brush.

3 Brush embroider (see glossary) the remaining areas, then pipe the dots (No.0).

4 Pipe shells around the cake-base (No.2).

5 Cut an 8 sectioned paper template and place onto the cake-top held down with a thin cake card. Pipe a line around the template edge (No.3).

6 Remove the template then pipe the further lines shown (No.2 and 1).

7 Fix the lace around the cake-top edge.

8 Cut out sugarpaste to the shape shown, using the template as a guide, and keep covered with polythene until required. Press one piece between polythene until thin.

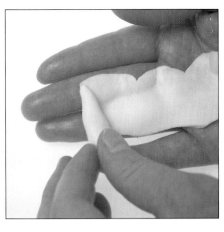

9 Remove the polythene, then roll-up the first section to form the bud.

10 Break the second section away.

11 Tuck that section inside the flap of the bud and roll-up to form the first petal. Break away the next section then tuck inside the flap.

12 Repeat until the required size of rose is made. Turn the tops of the petals outwards and at slightly different angles as shown.

13 Make as many roses as required then make and decorate into sprays, as shown.

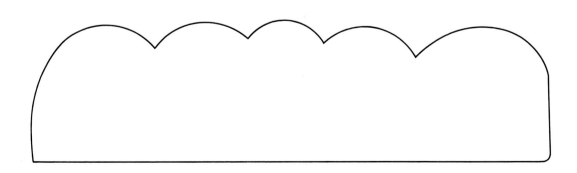

WEDDING FANTASY

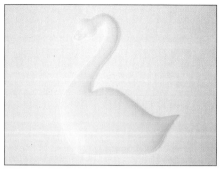

1 Coat the cakes with royal icing on separate boards. When dry stack together using thin cake cards between the layers, then seal together with a little royal icing around the bases. Coat board.

2 Outline the swan bodies onto non-stick paper with royal icing (No.1) then flood-in. Make as many as required in pairs together with their heart shaped bases. Leave to dry for 24 hours.

3 Pipe the appropriate swan wings on non-stick paper (No.3). Leave to dry for 24 hours.

4 Cut and fix mottled sugarpaste to the cake, to form the stream.

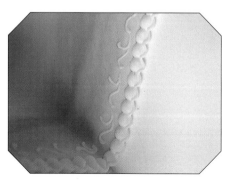

5 Pipe bulbs along each edge of the stream (No.2). Pipe a line over the bulbs then pipe tracery as shown (No.1).

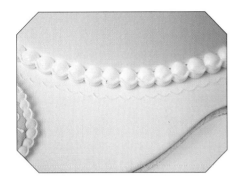

6 Pipe bulbs around the cake-bases (No.3). Pipe a line over the bulbs (No.2). Pipe curved lines beside the bulbs (No.1).

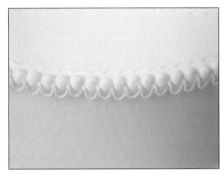

7 Pipe bulbs around the cake-top edges (No.3). Pipe loops below the bulbs (No.2). Pipe curved lines beside the bulbs (No.1).

8 Fix the swan bodies together, then onto the bases. Fix the wings (support if necessary). Leave to dry. Paint the beaks and eyes. Decorate with feathers and flowers and fix to the cake.

INGREDIENTS

7.5cm round cake (3in)
15cm round cake (6in)
25.5cm round cake (10in)
2.25k almond paste (4½lb)
2.25k royal icing (4½lb)
340g sugarpaste (12oz)
Blue, orange and black
  food colours

EQUIPMENT and DECORATIONS

7.5cm round cake card (3in)
15cm round cake card (6in)
35.5cm petal shaped cake
  board (14in)
Non-stick paper
Piping tubes No.1, 2 and 3
Feathers
Flowers
Board edge ribbon

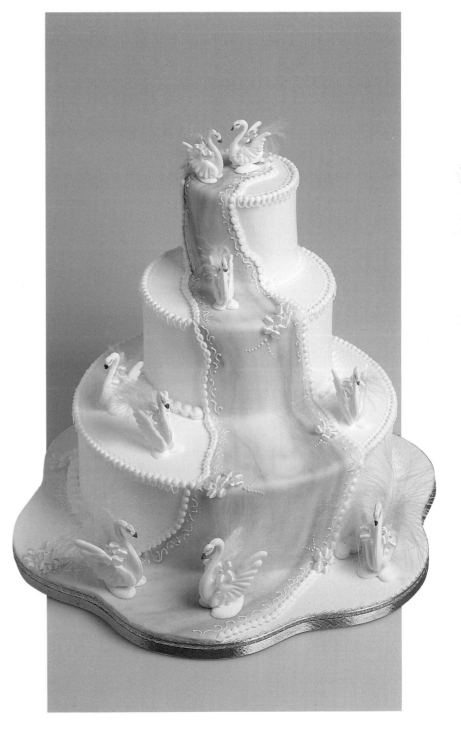

205

INGREDIENTS

20.5cm square cake (8in)
25.5cm square cake (10in)
30.5cm square cake (12in)
4.5k almond paste (10lb)
4.5k sugarpaste (10lb)
900g royal icing (2lb)
Pink food colour

EQUIPMENT and DECORATIONS

25.5cm round cake board (10in)
30.5cm round cake board (12in)
35.5cm round cake baord (14in)
10cm square cake board (4in)
15cm square cake board (6in)
20.5cm square cake board (8in)
Crimper
Piping tubes No.1, 2 and 42
Fuschia blossoms
Rings and doves
Medium frosted bells
Small frosted bells
Miniature horseshoes
Gypsophila (dried)
Narrow ribbons
Board edge ribbon

PREPARATION

Using the template as a guide, cut the sides of each cake to form the cushion shape. Then cover the cakes with sugarpaste. Cover the boards with sugarpaste and crimp around each edge. Leave the cakes and boards to dry for 24 hours.

1 Prepare the cakes. Fix a square board between the cake and covered round board. Fix ribbon. Pipe the shells (No.2) with royal icing.

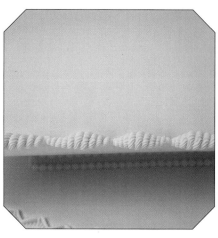

2 Pipe barrel scrolls around the edge of each cake (No.42).

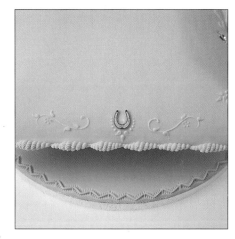

3 Fix a horseshoe on each cake-side then decorate with tracery (No.1).

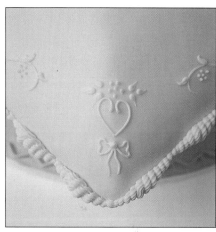

4 Pipe decorative pattern as shown on each corner (No.1).

5 Pipe a group of dropped lines between the scrolls then a bulb on the top to form the tassels (No.2).

6 Fix a fresh, crystallised or artificial flower to each cake corner. Decorate the cakes with bells, gypsophila and ribbons.

Sᴇᴘᴛᴇᴍʙᴇʀ WEDDING

INGREDIENTS

15cm round cake (6in)
23cm round cake (9in)
30.5cm round cake (12in)
3.5k almond paste (7lb)
3.5k royal icing (7lb)
Orange and green food colours

EQUIPMENT and DECORATIONS

20.5cm round cake board (8in)
28cm round cake board (11in)
40.5cm round cake board (16in)
Side scraper cut to shape
Non-stick paper
Piping tubes No.1, 2, 3, 4 and 57
Board edge ribbon

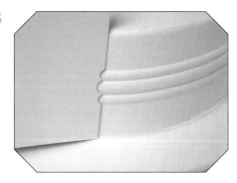

1 Coat the cakes and board with royal icing. On the final coat of each cake use a scraper cut to the pattern shown. Leave to dry for 24 hours.

2 Pipe flowers onto non-stick paper, using two colours of royal icing in the piping bag (No.57) for each tier.

3 Vary the sizes of the flowers according to the sizes of the cakes. Pipe the flowers centres (No.2). 36 required for each tier. Leave to dry for 24 hours.

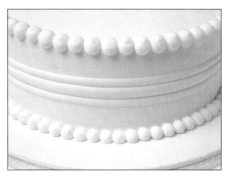

4 Pipe bulbs around the cake-top edge and base (No.4).

5 Overpipe each bulb with a smaller bulb (No.3).

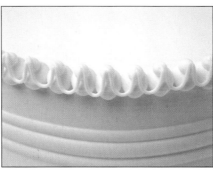

6 Pipe a loop to join each bulb (No.2).

7 Fix the flowers and pipe the stems (No.1) and then the leaves (No.2). Fix band around each board edge.

INGREDIENTS

20.5cm round cake (8in)
25.5cm round cake (10in)
30.5cm round cake (12in)
4k almond paste (8lb)
4k sugarpaste (8lb)
450g royal icing (8oz)
900g modelling paste (2lb)
Assorted food colours

EQUIPMENT and DECORATIONS

28cm round cake board (11in)
33cm round cake board (13in)
40.5cm round cake board (16in)
Cocktail stick
Piping tube No.1
Plastic dowling
Small blossom cutter
Asparagus fern (dried)
Narrow ribbon
Board edge ribbon

1 Cover cakes and boards with sugarpaste. Leave to dry 24 hours. Fix ribbon. Divide sides into 6 and mark equal curved lines. Cut, flute and fix sugarpaste frills.

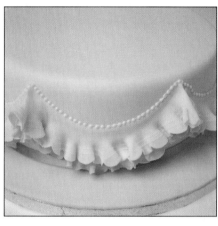

2 Cut, flute and fix a second sugarpaste frill. Pipe shells, with royal icing, along the top edge of each frill (No.1).

3 Pipe a floral pattern above each curve and around the board edge (No.1).

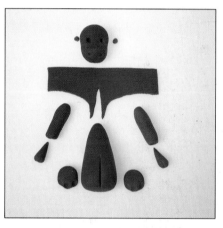

4 Using modelling paste, cut out and mould the various parts for the male hippo.

5 Fix the parts together, then push a length of dowling down the middle. Repeat steps 4 and 5 to make 1 groom and 3 ushers. Leave the top couple free of dowling.

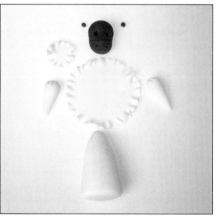

6 Cut out and mould various parts for female hippo. Fix parts together, then push a length of dowling down the middle. Decorate with flowers and fern.

7 Repeat step 5 to make 1 bride and 3 bridesmaids. Place onto cakes and push the dowling down to the boards. Cut the dowling to required height.

HEARTS DESIRE

1 Coat the cakes and boards with royal icing. Using the template as a guide, outline and flood-in with royal icing onto non-stick paper the pieces shown. Leave to dry for 24 hours.

2 When dry, remove the pieces shown from the paper, upturn and flood-in the tops. Leave to dry for 24 hours.

3 When dry assemble the pieces together, pipe the dots (No.1) and decorate with flowers.

4 Divide the cake into 16 sections pipe 'S' and 'C' scrolls around the cake-top and a line around the base (No.43).

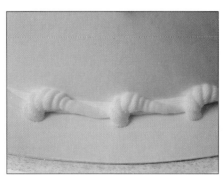

5 Pipe matching 'S' scrolls around the cake-base (No.43).

6 Overpipe all the scrolls (No.2) then pipe a line beside the cake-top scrolls (No.2).

7 Tilt the cake and pipe curved lines around the cake-side (No.1) then a scalloped line as shown (No.1).

8 Pipe heart shapes around the cake-side and scrolls around the board edge (No.1).

9 Pipe lines on each scroll as shown (No.1).

10 Pipe lines across the lace to form lattice (No.1). Decorate the cake with matching flowers and ribbons.

INGREDIENTS

15cm heart shaped cake (6in)
20.5cm heart shaped cake (8in)
25.5cm heart shaped cake (10in)
3k almond paste (6lb)
3k royal icing (6lb)
Lemon food colour

EQUIPMENT and DECORATIONS

23cm heart shaped cake board (9in)
28cm heart shaped cake board (11in)
33cm heart shaped cake board (13in)
Non-stick paper
Piping tubes No.1, 2 and 43
Flowers
Board edge ribbon

INGREDIENTS

20.5cm petal shaped cake (8in)
25.5cm petal shaped cake (10in)
30.5cm petal shaped cake (12in)
4k almond paste (8lb)
4k sugarpaste (8lb)
900g royal icing (2lb)
Cream and brown food colours

EQUIPMENT and DECORATIONS

25.5cm petal shaped cake
  board (10in)
30.5cm petal shaped cake
  board (12in)
35.5cm petal shaped cake
  board (14in)
Piping tubes 1, 2, 42, 43 and a very
  small petal tube
Rings and doves
Leaves
Board edge ribbon

1 Cover the cakes with sugarpaste and fix to the cake boards. Outline (No.2) and flood-in the cake board, with royal icing, as shown. Leave to dry for 24 hours.

2 Pipe small flowers onto non-stick paper with royal icing, using a very small petal piping tube. Pipe the dots (No.1). 200 required. Leave to dry for 24 hours.

3 Pipe shells around the cake-base (No.43).

4 Tilt the cake, then pipe scrolls around the cake-side (No.42).

5 Overpipe the scrolls (No.2).

6 Pipe lattice across the main scrolls (No.1).

7 Pipe curved lines around the cake-top edge (No.1). Fix the flowers to the lines, then pipe leaves (No.1). Decorate the cake with leaves, flowers and favours as required.

WEDDING BELLS

1 Cover the cakes with sugarpaste. Leave to dry for 24 hours. Cut and fix a sugarpaste frill around the base of each cake.

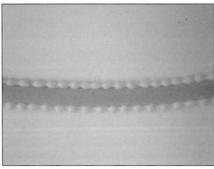

2 Cut and fix a narrow sugarpaste band along the top-edge of the frill together with a bow. Pipe shells with royal icing along each edge of the band (No.1).

3 Pipe the floral designs and rope lines as shown (No.1).

4 Pipe ribbon loops, bows, bells and floral sprays around the top of the cake (No.1).

5 Mould modelling paste into a cone, roll out the base then cut with a five petal shaped cutter. Place onto a sponge and press the centre of each petal with a bone tool to hollow out.

10cm bell shaped cake (4in) 5 required
15cm bell shaped cake (6in)
2.5k almond paste (5lb)
2.5k sugarpaste (5lb)
450g royal icing (1lb)
450g modelling paste (1lb)
Pink food colour

15cm round cake board (6in) 5 required
23cm round cake board (9in)
Bone modelling tool
Sponge
Piping tube No.1
Narrow ribbon

Five petal shaped cutter
Cocktail stick
Floral wire and tape
Stamens
Gypsophila (dried)
Board edge ribbon

6 Flute the edge of each petal with a cocktail stick. Cut out a second, flat petal shape, hollow out and flute.

7 Tape stamens to wire and insert into the fluted petals to form the flower.

8 Make a selection of flowers, form into sprays with a little gypsophila and ribbon loops, then fix to the cake as required.

ROSE CASCADE

15cm petal shaped cake (6in)
20.5cm petal shaped cake (8in)
25.5cm petal shaped cake (10in)
30.5cm petal shaped cake (12in)
3.5k almond paste (7½lb)
3.5k sugarpaste (7½lb)
450g royal icing (1lb)
1.5k sugarpaste (3lb) for
 the roses
Yellow food colour

40.5cm petal shaped cake
 board (16in)
15cm petal shaped cake card (6in)
20.5cm petal shaped cake card (8in)
25.5cm petal shaped cake
 card (10in)
Piping tubes No.2 and 3
Leaves
Gypsophila (dried)
Board edge ribbon

1 Cover the bottom cake and board with sugarpaste, then cover the other cakes on the cake cards. Leave to dry for 24 hours. Then stack the cakes as shown.

2 Pipe shells around each cake-base, with royal icing (No.3) to secure the cakes together.

3 Make sugarpaste roses and buds (see page 203). 15 large, 40 medium and 30 small roses plus 20 rose buds required. Leave to dry for 24 hours.

4 Start to fix the roses and buds to the cake, working from the top.

5 Continue fixing roses and buds to form a flowing cascade, finishing on the board.

6 Fix in gypsophila and leaves.

7 Pipe loops round the edge of each cake (No.2).

INDEX AND GLOSSARY

Brush embroidery. Pipe the pattern onto the cake or non-stick paper (No.1 or 2) a small area at a time using the recommended recipe. Brush the line immediately towards the design to smooth the icing, using a fine, damp (but not too wet) paint brush.

Cake-base. Where the bottom edges of the cake meet the cake board
Cake card – a thin cake board

Coated cake: a cake coated with buttercream or royal icing.

Colouring –
– Almond paste. Fold and mix colour into the almond paste.
– Buttercream. Mix colour into the buttercream after it has been made.
– Granulated sugar. Carefully add edible food colour to the sugar, mix thoroughly. Allow to dry for 24 hours.
– Modelling paste. Fold and mix the colour into the paste.
– Mottled paste: Where colouring is not fully mixed into the medium being used.
– Piping gel. Stir the colour into the gel.
– Royal icing. Mix colour into the royal icing after it has been made. Do not add blue to whiten the icing if pastel shades are required.
– Sugarpaste. Fold and mix the colour into the paste.

Covered cake: a cake covered with almond paste or sugarpaste

Decorative board covering can be wallpaper samples, or patterned paper, glued to the cake board. Use a cake card between the covering and the cake.

Stencils. These are easily available from craft shops. To make, trace design onto card. Cut out with scalpel or sharp knife. Place onto cake. Carefully spread softened royal icing over the stencil. Scrape off surplus with palette knife. Peel the stencil off in one continuous movement.

Stippling: Royal icing should be stippled with a clean, dry household sponge or palette knife.

**Templates. An aid for designs. To transfer templates:
1) Cut out card templates in sections. Place on cake-top and pipe around sections with royal icing. When dry, carefully remove the pieces once piped around. OR
2) Trace template onto greaseproof paper with a food-approved pen. Place design onto the cake-top. With a sharp pointed tool, press along the lines to leave an impression. OR
3) Retrace lines on back of design. Turn paper over and place on cake-top. Trace over with food-approved pen.**

TIERING CAKES

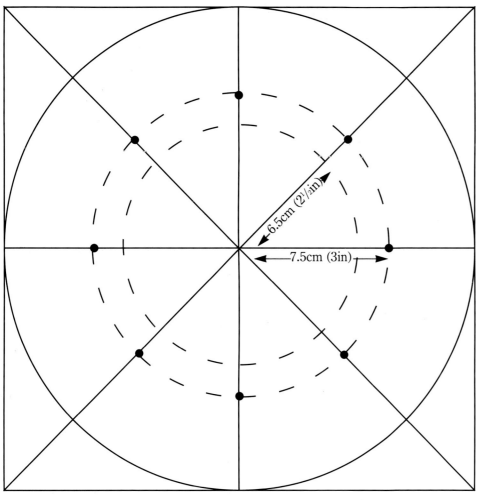

Not to scale

6.5cm (2½in)

7.5cm (3in)

For a 20.5cm (8in) cake, pillars should be positioned 6.5cm (2½in) from the centre. For a 25.5cm (10in) cake, pillars should be positioned 7.5cm (3in) from the centre. A square cake usually has 4 pillars which can be on the diagonal or cross, whichever suits the design best. A round cake usually has 3 pillars in a triangle, or four arranged in a circle.

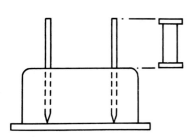

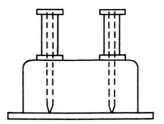

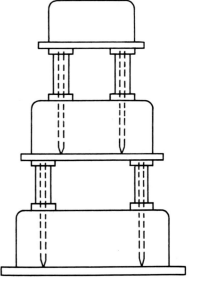

TIERING A SUGARPASTE-COVERED CAKE

1 Push food-approved rods into the cake to the board. Cut rods to height of pillar.

2 Place the pillars over the rods.

3 Assemble the cake, as required.

MARY FORD TITLES

Cake & Biscuit Recipes
ISBN: 0 946429 58 8   192 pages
Features over 60 cake and 100 biscuit recipes complete with full introductory pages for the beginner and "Mary's Tips" section to ensure better results.

Children's Birthday Cakes
ISBN: 0 946429 46 4   112 pages
The book to have next to you in the kitchen! Over forty new cake ideas for children's cakes with an introduction on cake making and baking to ensure the cake is both delicious as well as admired.

One Hundred Easy Cake Designs
ISBN: 0 946429 47 2   208 pages
Mary Ford has originated 100 cakes all of which have been selected for ease and speed of making. The ideal book for the busy parent or friend looking for inspiration for a special occasion cake.

A to Z of Cake Decorating
ISBN: 0 946429 52 9   208 pages
New dictionary style home cake decorating book with step-by-step examples covering the techniques and skills of the craft. Suitable for the beginner and enthusiast alike.

The New Book of Cake Decorating
ISBN: 0 946429 59 6   224 pages
The most comprehensive title in the Mary Ford list. It includes over 100 new cake designs and full descriptions of all the latest techniques.

Quick and Easy Cakes
ISBN: 0 946429 42 1   208 pages
The book for the busy mum. 99 new ideas for party and special occasion cakes.

Writing in Icing
ISBN: 0 946429 57 X   96 pages
Full step-by-step guide to over 50 writing styles showing both numbers and letters. The complete guide for the cake decorator to writing on cakes with icing.

Decorative Sugar Flowers for Cakes
ISBN: 0 946429 51 0   120 pages
33 of the highest quality handcrafted sugar flowers with cutter shapes, background information and appropriate uses.

Cake Recipes
ISBN: 0 946429 43 X   96 pages
Contains 60 of Mary's favourite cake recipes ranging from fruit cake to cinnamon crumble cake.

Biscuit Recipes
ISBN: 0 946429 50 2   96 pages
Nearly 100 biscuit and traybake recipes chosen for their variety and ease of making. Full introduction for beginners.

Home Baking with Chocolate
ISBN: 0 946429 54 5   96 pages
Over 60 tried and tested recipes for cakes, gateaux, biscuits, confectionery and desserts. The ideal book for busy mothers.

Novelty Cakes
ISBN: 0 946429 56 1   120 pages
Over 40 creative ideas to make a successful party. Introduction and basic recipes for beginners with full step-by-step guide to each cake design.

Making Cakes for Money
ISBN: 0 946429 44 8   120 pages
The complete guide to making and costing cakes for sale at stalls or to friends. Invaluable advice on costing ingredients and time accurately.

Kid's Cakes
ISBN: 0 946429 53 7   96 pages
33 exciting new Mary Ford designs and templates for children's cakes in a wide range of of mediums.

Jams, Chutneys and Pickles
ISBN: 0 946429 48 0   96 pages
Over 70 of Mary Ford's favourite recipes for delicious jams, jellies, pickles and chutneys with hints and tips for perfect results.

Wedding Cakes
ISBN: 0 946429 39 1   96 pages
For most cake decorators, the wedding cake is the most complicated item they will produce. This book gives a full step-by-step description of the techniques required and includes over 20 new cake designs.

BOOKS BY MAIL ORDER

Mary Ford operates a mail order service for all her step-by-step titles. If you write to Mary at the address below she will provide you with a price list and details. In addition, all names on the list receive information on new books and special offers. Mary is delighted, if required, to write a personal message in any book purchased by mail order.

Write to: Mary Ford,
            30 Duncliff Road,
            Southbourne, Bournemouth,
            Dorset. BH6 4LJ. U.K.